LOVIN' YOUR WIFE LIKE CHRIST WHEN YOU AIN'T NO JESUS

HOPE FOR ORDINARY MEN

Praise for *Lovin' Your Wife Like Christ*

"I was never a New England Patriot in my career and I always knew how lucky those players were . . . not only because of their championship seasons but the opportunity to have Paul Friesen as a personal mentor and Bible study leader and glean the never-ending stories and experiences that give him the ability to have a unique/unmatched comprehensive view on marriage. This book gives you that. It flows from genuine life story to story—and the applications to my life jump off the page."

MATT HASSELBECK
Former NFL quarterback and current ESPN analyst

"This is a book for all of us ordinary husbands who often fail at loving our wives, don't happen to be Jesus, and need some real encouragement. (I suspect I'm not the only one). With humility and humor, Paul Friesen encourages every husband who sincerely wants to do a better job at what often doesn't come naturally: loving his wife 'as Christ loved the church.' This book should be standard issue to all young husbands (and old ones, too)."

BENJAMIN C. WARF, MD
Professor of Neurosurgery, Harvard Medical School
Director of Neonatal and Congenital Anomaly Neurosurgery, and
Hydrocephalus and Spina Bifida Chair, Boston Children's Hospital

"There has been no voice and no example that has challenged us as a couple and me as a husband more than that of Paul Friesen's. In a world confused about marriage, his biblical advice, encouragement, and counsel has always turned me from feelings to truth, and from culture to Jesus. Whether newly married or a veteran in the game, this book will undoubtedly equip you to lead, love, and cherish your wife as you continue to grow into the man God has called you to be."

BENJAMIN WATSON
Veteran NFL Tight End, Speaker, Author of *Under Our Skin*

"Almost every book on marriage makes me feel worse. Paul always gives me hope! If you're ready for less guilt and more practical, honest help—from a real guy—this book is for you!"

RAY JOHNSTON
Lead Pastor, Bayside Churches, Granite Bay, CA

"Being a husband is one of God's greatest gifts to men. It is one of the most challenging things you will ever do, but also the most rewarding thing (second only to knowing Jesus). With a practical, relatable, and reliable voice, Paul Friesen has hit the nail on the head once again. *Lovin' Your Wife Like Christ When You Ain't No Jesus* will encourage you to become the husband God has called you to be through the example of Christ. My wife and I are thankful for Paul's guidance and encouragement over the years. Now you too can benefit from his mentoring through this book."

MATTHEW SLATER
11-Year Veteran New England Patriots, Special Teams Captain
Two-time Super Bowl champion, seven-time Pro Bowler

"I so appreciate Paul Friesen and thank God for his steady, ongoing investment into men over many years. Almighty God has used him possibly more than any man I know to build Godly husbands and fathers, and this book is one of the results of that investment. Grab this book and grab a friend and devour it together—not for you, but for those who you love the most!"

BRIAN DOYLE
Founder and President, Iron Sharpens Iron

"This a great reminder for all men that even though we don't always get marriage right, there is always hope for improvement. Paul is a leader and a teacher, and will mentor us through this journey. As I read this book I was reminded that we typically don't drift toward a successful marriage, we make it happen. This book is very much worth your time and effort."

JIM BURNS, PhD
President, HomeWord
Author of *Creating an Intimate Marriage, Closer,*
The First Few Years of Marriage, and *Getting Ready for Marriage*

"The book is a Game Changer and a win-win for both husband and wife. It is a book I will be referencing and re-reading a lot because there is so much in it for us men to follow. It had me laughing at a lot of parts and tearing up at other parts, knowing I am not alone. And it felt at times that you were speaking right to me."

KEN GAUDET
Upton, Massachusetts

"I just finished reading the manuscript *Lovin' Your Wife Like Christ When You Ain't No Jesus* and really like it. As expected, it was easy to read, with clear teaching points backed by scripture, great illustrations, and humor. I like how each chapter is laid out: very organized, no rambling, and right to the point. I appreciated that each chapter ends with highlights (a man's favorite section!), discussion questions for the guys, a game plan to help the guys get 'unstuck.' And I especially appreciated 'A Word from the Wives.' I highly recommend this book to any guy wanting to take his marriage to the next level."

JOHN NUGENT
President, Joni and Friends

"Paul Friesen is that rare author who successfully combines truth and grace, deep insights with down-to-earth advice, and God's word with a lifetime of experience. *Lovin' Your Wife Like Christ* is the kind of book that you will highlight and re-read, that will lead to deeper conversations with your spouse, and that will have you sending copies to your friends. Paul is one of the best authors and speakers on marriage that I know. If you are seeking an author/speaker/expert, whether for your own personal growth or for a small group experience, you will want to have this book. In it you will find an 'increased sense of God's pleasure in you, rather than His disappointment.' Marriages can be a struggle for many people, and loving our spouses like Christ is a noble endeavor. Paul gives us a game plan on how to do it. His book is an engaging, insightful, and professional look into the most intimate of all of our relationships—our marriages—that is based on Paul's extensive expertise, practical research, and his personal journey. For those of you who desire authentic intimacy, biblical insights, and practical ways on how to love your wife like Christ—you are looking at the best book you can find on this topic."

DR. CHRIS GRACE
Center for Marriage and Relationships, Biola University, La Mirada, CA

"If our marriages are a living metaphor of the Gospel, men, we need to represent Christ's love to the world in how we love our wives. Consider this book your field manual for how to grow in that privileged sacred trust. This should be mandatory reading before every marriage license is handed out! It will be mandatory reading for any man married in our church!"

GARY L. GADDINI
Lead Pastor, Peninsula Covenant Church, Redwood City, CA

"When you read Paul Friesen it's like chatting over a cup of coffee. *Lovin' Your Wife Like Christ When You Ain't No Jesus* is Paul at his accessible best. With his trade-mark style he dives into every husband's mind, validates his fears, and then brings Jesus and Scriptural truth to bear in a way that makes us want to obey. If you're serious about crafting a marriage that is both satisfying and glorifying, read this book. You'll find buckets of hope, and some easy first steps. I highly recommend it!"

DR. DAVID W. HEGG
Senior Pastor, Grace Baptist Church, Santa Clarita, CA

"Paul Friesen combines his dry wit and direct approach with decades of study and counseling experience in *Lovin' Your Wife Like Christ When You Ain't No Jesus*. This book is an engaging, authentic look at who Jesus is, how He loves His people, and what He calls His people to do: become more like Him in marriage, and reflect His glory through that marriage. Paul encourages and guides us as husbands to better know and understand Christ with the aim of better loving and understanding our wives. With practical advice for men, and even a bit for women, this refreshing book captures our attention with humor and heartfelt anecdotes while inspiring us to love our spouses the way Christ loves us. Paul's book makes Jesus more approachable and the goal of loving more like Him, achievable."

BILL BACHMAN
Husband to Christi and father of two sons, San Jose, CA

"I just finished your manuscript. It is fantastic and what all of us men need to hear. You are spot on and it is an easy read for those of us who are not readers. Thank you for sharing this with me. It was an honor to see this before the public. I can't wait to purchase this book."

DAVID WATTS
Sacramento, CA

About the *Bonus* chapter for wives . . .

"This book is a fantastic guide to loving our husbands well, as God desires!"

ELISABETH HASSELBECK
Daughter of God, wife to Tim, mom of three fun children
Author of *Point of View*

"While *Lovin' Your Wife Like Christ* is primarily focused on advising men to approach their marriages in Christ-like, meaningful ways, I found the bonus chapter for wives to be thought-provoking. Paul also challenges wives to bring Christ to the center of their marriages. Just as he is unswerving in his biblical advice to husbands in previous chapters, Paul holds the mirror up to any of us who think the only problem in our marriages is our husbands, and calls us to approach our daily interactions in a Christ-honoring way. He humorously nudges wives to love their husbands with grace, respect, and understanding."

CHRISTI BACHMAN
Wife to Bill and mom of two sons, San Jose, CA

"I love the 'Bonus' chapter for women! I can't began to tell you how many times I've heard women complain about their husbands without realizing that they themselves are a huge part of why they are so dissatisfied in their marriage. This chapter is a profound reminder of the simple things we wives can do to uplift and respect our husbands so we can have a more loving and fulfilling marriage."

DINA ANDERSON
Sacramento, California

"I found myself completely engaged in each point Paul was making in this chapter and found the chapter ended too quickly. He does not hold back and—Ha!—actually crosses the line into what I think we normally set up as a barrier to someone speaking into our married lives. His real life experiences with couples help to expose the truth of the relationship killers that I find I must admit to myself. Yet I am energized to make immediate changes and not discouraged. Paul gives easy suggestions to positively impact my exact situations with only a few simple words or actions."

SARAH HASSELBECK
Wife of Matt Hasselbeck and mother of three great kids

LOVIN'
YOUR
WIFE
LIKE
CHRIST
WHEN
YOU
AIN'T
NO
JESUS

HOPE FOR
ORDINARY MEN

Paul Friesen

Home Improvement Ministries
Bedford, Massachusetts

Lovin' Your Wife Like Christ When You Ain't No Jesus

Cover design: David Foglesong
Book design and production: Barbara Steele
Copy editing: Guy Steele

ISBN: 978-1-936907-13-7

Published by Home Improvement Ministries.
For information on other H.I.M. resources, please contact:
   Home Improvement Ministries
   213 Burlington Road, Suite 101-B
   Bedford, MA 01730
E-mail inquiries: info@HIMweb.org
Website: www.HIMweb.org

Printed in the United States of America.   12-10/18TPS2000

To my wife of 42 years—

Virginia

Thank you for continuing to love me well,
even when I often fall so short of loving you like Christ.

Contents

Foreword

This won't be a long foreword. We need to get right down to business, and that means diving into what Paul Friesen has to say. It's worthwhile, though, to say something that Paul won't. Or can't. Or shouldn't.

1. I have a hyper-sensitive B.S. detector (I hope it's okay I say "B.S." instead of baloney, but take your pick.)

   But I will listen to Paul.

   My sensitivity is due to my years of working in "Christian entertainment" as a radio host, and my background growing up in the church, being confronted up-close with the worst kinds of hypocrisy.

   Anyone with my past is naturally always looking around suspiciously, squinting and wondering, "Is this real or not?"

2. I know Paul Friesen. I know his wife and family. They are the reason you should read this. My wife, Carolyn, and I listen to what he says. His words are not idle words, borne of a desire to be famous or significant. He's not needy.

   He's what I want to be when I finally grow up. He's a listener. He's patient. He's other-focused. I think a lot of us yearn for that; for an older, thoughtful man who has earned the right to speak into our lives.

Only God knows the status of someone else's heart, and Paul is a fallen human like the rest of us. But when I see how his grown daughters love and respect him, and how his wife does as well, and how they all fairly sparkle with confidence and love for others, well . . . I want to learn from this guy.

And now, here's our chance . . .

Brant Hansen
Nationally syndicated radio host, and
Author of *Unoffendable* and *Blessed Are the Misfits*

Acknowledgments

I started writing *Lovin' Your Wife Like Christ When You Ain't No Jesus* in October of 2014, over four years ago. If books get better with age, this will be a dandy.

First I want to thank Wes and Anna Welker, who graciously let me live in their home in Fort Lauderdale, Florida, for a week as I cranked out 80% of the book—and then the crankshaft froze.

During these four years, a host of men have been involved in reading and commenting on the various renditions of the manuscript. Special thanks to you for your feedback and suggestions:

Dave Sherman, Don Davis, Dane Looker, Scott Shaull, Nate King, John Nugent, Ryan Plosker, Brent Slezak, Jack Harvey, Gabe Garcia, Nate Solder, Doug Macrae, Gary Gaddini, Bill Bachman, Kyle Keldsen, Wes Welker, Matthew Slater, Derek Johnson, Wai Wong, Dan Robbins, Ryan Plosker, Carl Blatchley, Richard Hendricks, Guy Steele, Dan Yardley, David Leach, Grant Williams, Johnny Potter, Ken Gaudet, Sebastian Volmer, Rob Warren, Brian Doyle, Jim Burns, Ray Johnston, Benjamin Watson, Danny Oertli, David Watts, Don Hasselbeck, Kent Copley

I want to especially thank Wai Wong, Don Davis, Brant Hansen, Kent Copley, and Bill Bachman for their extensive input.

I truly believe none of our books would be a reality were it not for the expert editing and formatting of Barbara and Guy Steele. Your generous contribution to this project and many others is enormous.

David Foglesong's patience and creativity through the various renditions of the book cover are deeply appreciated.

The book would never have become a reality without the support of my girlfriend and wife of 42 years, Virginia. Thanks for believing in the book, even when I did not.

Lastly, my deepest acknowledgment is to the One who is Christ to His bride, the Church. I am deeply humbled, Jesus, that you continue to love me, even when I am far from loving you or my bride like you love.

Introduction

If you wake up each morning to a wife who greets you with "Darling, I am the luckiest woman in the world to be married to you. You understand me and love me so well. I can't think of anything I would change in you, even if I could . . .", if your kids greet you with "Dad, you are the best. Thanks for always knowing what to do, for never getting angry, and for modeling for us the love of our Heavenly Father . . . ", or if you seldom feel like you fail God and seldom feel like a loser as a Christian man, then this book is likely not for you.

If, however, you want to be a better husband, father, and follower of Christ, but often feel like you miss the mark, I think this book might be for you, and I can assure you, you are not alone. If I were to interview 100 husbands, I believe I would find that over 75 of them would attest to often feeling like they are a disappointment to their wives, to their children, and to God. The other 25 simply have an overinflated view of themselves. To add to this sense of failure, the best-known passage on marriage in the Bible, and one our wives have put to memory, instructs us as husbands to *"love your wives, as Christ loved the church . . . "* Now that's a bar we can barely see, let alone reach. What husband can love his wife like Christ? Who do our wives think we are? Jesus?

Back when we were dating, it was hard to imagine some of the challenges we would eventually face in marriage. She seemed so excited to be with us and we seemed to "get her." Fast forward to marriage and maybe you can identify with a story from my life.

It was Mother's Day and my wife Virginia had a stomach bug, so we abandoned our usual Mother's Day tradition where I would make a simple breakfast and the girls would serve it to their mom in bed. We went in to see what we could do to help celebrate the day or make her feel better. "Please, don't do anything for me, just go to church and I will rest at home." So we went to church, then returned home to see how she was feeling. As we walked into the room, she burst into tears. "It's Mother's Day, and I thought you might at least bring me flowers or do something." Now, when she said, "Please don't do anything for me," I thought she meant, "Please don't do anything for me." Sometimes it is challenging to be a husband. During these times it is easy to let our specific "miss" or "failure" define us and thus easy to get quite discouraged. I call these "snapshot moments."

In the life of King David, for instance, the snapshot could be his adultery and having Bathsheba's husband murdered. For the apostle Paul, it could be his participation in the stoning of Christians. For Peter, it would be his 3-time denial of knowing Christ. For me, it could be the day I walked into a porn shop wearing a shirt that said "Jesus is Lord."

Instead of defining our lives through these snapshots, may I suggest we consider our lives as more of a video. For King David, the video was God identifying him as "a man after God's own heart." For the apostle Paul, the video was of a man who wrote, "For me, to live is Christ and to die is gain." For Peter, it would be the life of a man who served Jesus by powerfully building His Church. For me . . . well, the camera is still rolling.

Forget the snapshot that your father, employer, teacher, or wife took of you. Come, let's make a video in which we finish well and someday hear, "Well done" (not perfectly done) "good and faithful servant. . . . Enter into the joy of your master." (Matthew 25:21) That's what I want. How about you?

DESIRED OUTCOME

I have four hopes as you read this book. First, I trust you will realize you are not alone. As you read the stories, perhaps you will laugh as you see yourself in many of them.

Second, I trust you will have an increased sense of God's pleasure in you, rather than His disappointment.

Third, I want you to have hope rather than despair for your marriage and family.

Finally, I want you to gain some very practical and achievable tips on how to love your wife like Christ.

So, let's get to it and see how we can be the man God has called us to be and love well the wife He has given us, even when we "ain't no Jesus."

Paul Friesen
December 2018

A WORD FROM THE WIVES

Starting in chapter four, I will include the responses wives sent in when I surveyed them about their marriage and what would improve their relationship with their husband. As you will see, our wives are not quite as "high needs" as we often make them out to be. What came through again and again is they want us as husbands to take initiative in our marriage and simply show them we value them.

HIGHLIGHTS

These are bullet points at the end of every chapter to help us remember what we just read, or to read first to decide if you want to read the chapter.

GAME PLAN

A few concrete suggestions for what you might do to implement the material in the chapter. They are just that, suggestions. Some may work for you, some may not. You may have other ideas to implement that work much better for you. The main idea is "do something" each week to strengthen your marriage.

TALKIN' WITH THE BROTHERS

Suggested questions to use in a small group with other men. I can't emphasize enough the benefit of inviting other men to enter into this journey with you. Gather a few guys together and use these questions and see how God will meet you. Seek a more mature man that you look up to and ask him to lead your study.

DISCUSSING THE WORD

A passage and set of questions to help individuals or those in a small group to get into God's word around the focus of the preceding chapter. The hope is that all will renew their appreciation for the relevance of God's word and its application to everyday life.

1

Love My Wife Like Christ?

Oh, man, I'm going to need some help!

In 2012, New England Patriots tight-end receiver Wes Welker and his soon-to-be-wife, Anna, asked me to officiate at their June wedding on the top of Aspen Ridge in Colorado. While in the reception line, Wes re-introduced me to one of his groomsmen, Tom Brady. I had met Tom once after a game in 2001, but was not sure he would remember me, and I was right. Since we were "hanging out in Aspen together," I thought I would take advantage of this opportunity and ask Tom to confirm a story I'd heard about him.

The story was that when Tom was in 8th grade, a coach named Tom Martinez taught him how to pass a football. Even after three Super Bowl victories and a Hall of Fame career, Martinez would often call Brady and critique him. What was more amazing to me was that I was told that Tom welcomed those calls. So while I was in line at the reception, I asked Tom if the story were true and if so, how he felt about the calls.

"Yes, it is true, and I did welcome the calls."

"Why would you welcome someone critiquing you?" I asked.

"Easy," he said, "I knew he was *for* me."

IMPROVING YOUR GAME

If we're honest with ourselves, like Tom Brady, most of us need a really good "coach." Most of us feel we are a disappointment to our wives and need someone who will help us improve our game, a coach who is for us. Unfortunately for many of us, our experiences with coaches have not been positive. Perhaps you had a coach that used fear or intimidation as his motivational tactic. He was constantly yelling and pointing out what you were doing wrong. It seems he wanted you to feel like you were only one mistake away from being cut from the team. Some of us were raised with that view of Jesus—a view that focused on the things we did wrong and the fear of what would happen if we didn't perform correctly.

WE HAVE A COACH UNLIKE ANY OTHER COACH— ONE WHO IS TRULY FOR US, UNDERSTANDS US, AND DOES NOT THREATEN TO "KICK US OFF THE TEAM" EVERY TIME WE BLOW IT.

Many of us thought, from our dating experience, that we would finally be marrying someone that would be a cheerleader, someone that would always be for us, but found out after marriage she at times seems more like a critical coach than an enthusiastic cheerleader. Try as we do, we often don't seem to get it right and sometimes live in fear of "getting cut" or at least being relegated to the bench.

I don't think the problem for most of us is that we don't give a darn and are basically lazy. I believe deep in the heart of every man is the longing to hear, from those he loves, especially his wife, something similar to the words Jesus heard from the one He loved: *"This is my beloved Son, with whom I am well pleased."* And yet many of us grew up with, and still live with, a sense that we are not only not pleasing, but are a disappointment to, those we love and want to please.

The magnitude of feeling like we are missing the mark reminds me of my fourth grade teacher, Mrs. Humble. She wrote on the back of my report card, where only parents were intended to see, "Paul is a nice boy; he is just slow." I knew that Mrs. Humble was not talking about my athletic abilities. She was saying, "Your son is nice, but he is challenged intellectually." For the next 30 years, when I did well at anything academically, I would think, "That's odd—I'm dumb." When I was in seminary at age 42, I was tricked into taking an IQ test. I had refused to take them earlier, reasoning that it is better to think you are dumb than to know you are dumb. But I found out from the IQ test that I actually have a decent IQ, but have a huge learning disability. All of a sudden, the past three decades of my life made sense. For 30 years Mrs. Humble's words had "defined" me— and I didn't even like her! But, like a coach, she was an influential person in my life, and her words stuck.

For some of us our wife has become our "Mrs. Humble," who seems to remind us in various ways that we are just not cutting it as a husband and father, let alone as a follower of Christ. Some of us came into marriage with a history of feeling like a disappointment to our parents or others in authority over us and actually believed that finally, in marriage, we would have someone who did not view us as a disappointment. We are all in need of a supportive spouse and a coach who will encourage us to be the men God designed us to be.

Well, we have a coach unlike any other coach—One who is truly for us, understands us, and does not threaten to "kick us off the team" every time we blow it. Make no mistake, He is a coach who expects excellence, because He wants us to win in this thing called marriage and life, but somehow He creates an atmosphere where we want to run to Him instead of away from Him when we fail to make the play.

> *For we do not have a high priest who is unable to sympathize with our weaknesses, but one who in every respect has been tempted as we are, yet without sin. Let us then with confidence draw near to the throne of grace, that we may receive mercy and find grace to help in time of need.* —Hebrews 4:15–16

Did you hear that? We have a Coach who—even though He never failed—"gets" us. He understands our temptations. He knows we will fail at times, and when we do, instead of judgment and condemnation, He extends mercy and grace in our time of need.

YOU ARE NOT THE ONLY ONE

My favorite illustration of all time is set during the Great Depression. A father was out of work and his family was nearly starving. One day, as he was walking, he came across a sign at the local zoo that read, "Help Wanted." He went to the owner of the zoo, introduced himself, and then immediately said, "I'll take the job."

The owner objected, "But you have no idea what the job is!"

"It doesn't matter," replied the gentleman, "I need a job."

The owner then explained that their gorilla had died, and it was the main attraction to the zoo. He had a gorilla outfit and needed someone to "be the gorilla". The man was hired, and though it took a few days for him to get the hang of it, eventually he was better than the real gorilla. People were flocking to the zoo to see the antics of the "gorilla." Well, one day the "gorilla" got a bit overconfident and climbed up into a tree overhanging the lion's cage—but a limb broke, and he fell to the ground. The lion growled and approached the "gorilla," who slowly retreated unti he hit the back of the cage. Believing his life was about to end, he yelled, *"Help!"*—and the lion whispered, "Be quiet! Do you want us both to lose our jobs?"

Too often we are like the gorilla: we realize that we are not what we appear to be, yet we assume everyone else *is* just as they appear. After living over six decades and counseling myriads of men, let me assure you: none of us is as we appear to be. We all struggle in various ways to be the husbands God has called us to be. Our mistake is putting on the masks and acting like we have it all together. Not only do we rob ourselves of getting the support we need, we also discourage others as they look at our "masks" and think, "I wish I were like him; I bet he never fails like I do."

One of the great benefits of meeting with a group of authentic men is realizing we are not alone. It is helpful to know we are not the only ones who struggle, but even more helpful to hear how God has helped other men in their struggle to walk more obediently and

Love My Wife Like Christ?

faithfully with the Lord. Some groups, however, help us feel like everyone's doing it but do little to help us grow. I call such a group a "Denny's group." It consists of a group of men who meet for breakfast every Monday morning at 6 am, and the conversations go like this: "How did your week go?" "Pretty good." "How are you doing in the area of sexual purity?" "Better." "That's wonderful . . . anyone tried the pancakes here?"

In a real accountability group, questions are asked that specifically deal with your area of struggle: "Did you look at anything sexually explicit this week?" or "Did you drink any alcohol this week?" or "What did you do to strengthen your marriage?" or "How many days did you have a time with the Lord in His word?" The questions are tailored to you and they are very specific. Make sure your men's group is not just empathetic, but prophetic as it speaks God's truth into your life and holds you accountable in a way that will bring about change.

NOW THAT YOU HAVE A COACH AND A TEAM

With a coach even better than Tom Martinez, and a team who all want you to be everything you can be, you're ready to become an even better husband. Make no mistake: when we are asked to be "imitators of God" or to love our wives "as Christ loved the Church," we are being asked to do something that will stretch us. Yet God knows we will all fail at times and has made provision for us to be forgiven and get back in the game. The difference between those who make it in the NFL and those who don't often has to do with how they respond to failure and how they respond to their coach. We have seen too many very talented players who have missed out on fulfilling careers because they quit and/or refused to listen to good coaching.

We *will* fail at times. Get up and don't quit. We have a great coach who wants us to be better husbands, fathers, and followers of Him. He knows that to the degree we imitate Him, we will be fully alive as we were created to be—and in turn, we will more fully glorify the Lord. In the words of Saint Irenaeus, "The glory of God is man fully alive."

25

CHAPTER HIGHLIGHTS

► Most men feel a sense of failure at times and believe they are a disappointment to their wife, to their children, and to God.

► We often let others define us and thus live with a sense of failure.

► We all need a life coach.

► When you know your coach is *for* you, you welcome his critique.

► We have a "coach" who gets us and understands our temptations, and still urges us to come to Him.

► Having men who hold us accountable and give us strategies to improve is critical to our growth.

GAME PLAN

○ Find a Bible and read the first two chapters of the Gospel of Mark to start getting a view of who this man Jesus is.

○ If you pray, thank God that He loves you, period. Thank Him that He understands you.

TALKIN' WITH THE BROTHERS

1. Go around, and share briefly your life story.

2. If your wife were permitted only one word, what word would she use to describe you?

3. What word would you like your wife to use to describe you?

4. If you have children, what word would they use to describe you?

5. What word do you think God has to describe you?

6. Do you have a "Tom Martinez" in your life? If so, describe him.

7. What is your view of Jesus as your coach?

8. What one "take-away" do you have from this chapter to encourage you?

DISCUSSING THE WORD

[14]Since then we have a great high priest who has passed through the heavens, Jesus, the Son of God, let us hold fast our confession. [15]For we do not have a high priest who is unable to sympathize with our weaknesses, but one who in every respect has been tempted as we are, yet without sin. [16]Let us then with confidence draw near to the throne of grace, that we may receive mercy and find grace to help in time of need. —Hebrews 4:14–16

1. Why do we like having a coach who has experienced our sport or field of work?

2. Why are we encouraged to "draw near" to our coach, Jesus, when we are tempted or have failed?

3. What are we assured of if we run *to* rather than *away from* Jesus in our time of need?

2

I Need a Model to Imitate

Sometimes good models are hard to find

LEARNING FROM THE EXPERT

I grew up in central California on a rural farm. Most nights I went outside and listened to baseball games on our car radio, since for some reason the radio in our house could not pick up the games. Night after night I would head outside and listen to Vince Scully announce games for what I believed was the greatest team of all time, the Los Angeles Dodgers! Night after night I would listen as Wally Moon would get up to bat, and Don Drysdale and Sandy Koufax would take the mound, pitching as no one else could. When a game was on television I would be mesmerized as I watched every move these players made. The next day I'd go outside and "hit like Wally Moon" and "pitch like Sandy Koufax." Well, not exactly, but I would mimic what I observed in these "god-like" athletes. I knew I would never actually hit as well as Wally Moon, or pitch like Sandy Koufax, but I would imitate them as best I could.

I never had the privilege of meeting any of these legends nor attending the camps they ran for young athletes, but if I had, I imagine they would never have ridiculed me for not being "as good" as they were. They would encourage me as they saw me attempting to imitate them and would urge me to be the very best I could be.

THE PERFECT MENTOR

In Chapter 1 we looked at Jesus as our coach. Let's switch the metaphor and look at Him as our mentor, one who lived among us. John 1:14 says, *"And the Word* [Jesus] *became flesh and dwelt among us."* We have a mentor who bats a thousand and pitches nothing but no-hitters. While He realizes that we will never bat a thousand nor pitch nothing but no-hitters, He does call us to "learn from him." He doesn't want us to be weighed down with a sense of failure, but to find hope as we seek to imitate Him. He realizes we are often weary, tired, and in need of a break. He says to us in His word:

> *Come to me, all who labor and are heavy laden, and I will give you rest. Take my yoke upon you, and learn from me, for I am gentle and lowly in heart, and you will find rest for your souls. For my yoke is easy, and my burden is light."* —Matthew 11:28-30

Isn't that a great mentor to listen to? Jesus isn't like some of our fathers, who may have never been pleased with us or who always pushed us, saying if we tried harder we could have done better. He isn't like some wives who never seem to be pleased and continue to add "burdens" of failure to our backs. No, He is calling us to come to Him, to learn from Him, and to find rest in Him. He is the one we are called to imitate. As Ephesians 5:1 says, *"Therefore be imitators of God, as beloved children."*

The passage does not say "Therefore be God." Nor are we called to be "Christ" to our wives. We are called to love our wives "as Christ loved the Church." We are called to be "imitators of God." Children are not to imitate parents, teachers, or athletes out of fear or dread, but out of admiration and respect. This is what we are called to do, to imitate Christ as the "perfect husband" with excitement about what we might learn from Him.

MOST IMPROVED PLAYER

Over the years, as the dad of three very athletic daughters, I have sat through many an award ceremony at the end of the season. I have been on the edge of my seat at many ceremonies waiting for the

Most Valuable Player award to be announced, and sometimes it was awarded to one of our daughters. Despite my natural interest in the MVP award, I must admit that I was equally captivated as the coach announced the Most Improved Player. These players never expected to get the MVP award, but the smiles on their faces often surpassed the MVP-winner's smile because they knew that while they had not started in the top of the pack, they had worked hard, watched diligently, and improved greatly.

> **JESUS DOESN'T WANT US TO BE WEIGHED DOWN WITH A SENSE OF FAILURE, BUT TO FIND HOPE AS WE SEEK TO IMITATE HIM.**

Each of you reading this book has a different story. Some of you have come from supportive families and have observed marriages that, though not perfect, have reflected God's design for relationships. Others of you, just like a good friend of mine, have come from backgrounds void of a positive model of a Godly marriage and family.

My friend came from a pagan home. His parents divorced when he was 4 years old. When he was 8, his mother gave him marijuana for the first time, and when he was 10, she sent him off to live in a commune. Today he is married to his first wife and has three children who have been raised to know the security of an intact home. He is a good father, and his children know no other model. He continues to learn what it means to be a Godly husband and father, and while he certainly has not done it all perfectly, he gets my award as most improved.

Since we each enter marriage from different backgrounds, it is encouraging to know that Jesus understands the road we have been traveling and doesn't expect each of our journeys to be the same. In Matthew 25, Jesus tells a parable about some men who were given talents to invest while their master was away. One man was given five talents, another two, and another one. The man who was given one talent did nothing with it and received the displeasure of his master. What really interests me in this story, however, is the response of the master to the servants who were given five talents and two talents.

> *"And he who had received the five talents came forward, bringing five talents more, saying, 'Master, you delivered to me five talents; here, I have made five talents more.' His master said to him, 'Well done, good and faithful servant. You have been faithful over a little; I will set you over much. Enter into the joy of your master.' And he also who had the two talents came forward, saying, 'Master, you delivered to me two talents; here, I have made two talents more.' His master said to him, 'Well done, good and faithful servant. You have been faithful over a little; I will set you over much. Enter into the joy of your master.'"* —Matthew 25:20–23

What intrigues me about this story is that the master has the exact same response to the two servants, even though the amounts of the returns were different. I don't know about you, but that takes a load off my shoulders. Jesus is saying, "I know what hand you were dealt. My desire is that you will take what you have, grow it, and use it well."

IT TAKES ONLY ONE GENERATION TO CHANGE A LEGACY

One of my best friends married when he was just out of college. He and his wife both came from extremely dysfunctional homes. Both families were plagued by alcoholism and divorce. The situation was so bad for his wife that soon after they were married, her brother came to live with them because her mom could not take care of him. Eventually, she adopted her brother—so, legally, her brother is her son. If ever a couple had a reason to fail, this is the couple. They have been married now for over 20 years and have three daughters of their own. If you met them for the first time, you might guess that they both grew up in strong Christian homes, were home-schooled their whole lives, met each other at a Christian university, and basically never experienced any pain or heartache. That's not how it went—but because of their choices to learn from Jesus and to be intentional in finding mentors in marriage and parenting, this is a totally different family one generation later. Their daughters know nothing of the destruction of the homes in which their parents were raised. Their experience has always been that of being raised in a family that loves the Lord and each other. It takes only one generation to change the legacy of a family.

"FATHERS" WHO AREN'T IN HEAVEN

Some of us grew up without a model of what it means to be a Godly husband and dad. In addition to the model of Christ, it is helpful to have the encouragement and modeling of a man or two we can learn from. One wife wrote,

> I wish my husband had been brought up in a family with a father who knew Jesus personally. I am, however, so thankful that he was intentional about exposing himself regularly to a couple of men in our church. I am eternally grateful to these two men who helped my husband learn what it meant to be a God-honoring husband and father. Even though he did not "start well," he and we finished well before God took him home.

CALL TO EXCELLENCE WITHOUT THE GUILT

If anyone in scripture could identify with the challenge of wanting to do it right but at times missing the mark, it would be Peter. Peter is the one who told Christ that though everyone else would deny Him, he would not—and soon afterward denied knowing Christ three times. It is therefore especially poignant when he challenges us not to conform to our past, but to seek to honor Christ in the present.

> *As obedient children, do not be conformed to the passions of your former ignorance, but as he who called you is holy, you also be holy in all your conduct, since it is written, "You shall be holy, for I am holy."*
> —*1 Peter 1:14–16*

Scripture creates tension for Christ-followers; it calls us to holiness, while realizing that, apart from Christ, we will never experience it. It calls us to be conformed to the image of Christ, but realizes we will never be fully conformed until we are with Him. The apostle John challenges us to *"walk in the light, as He is in the light . . ."* which is a life without sin—and then immediately states that if we say we have no sin, we are liars, which is sin.

This is the message we have heard from him and proclaim to you, that God is light, and in him is no darkness at all. If we say we have fellowship with him while we walk in darkness, we lie and do not practice the truth. But if we walk in the light, as he is in the light, we have fellowship with one another, and the blood of Jesus his Son cleanses us from all sin. If we say we have no sin, we deceive ourselves, and the truth is not in us. —1 John 1:5–8

So we have our mentor and example, Jesus Christ, who calls us to holiness, yet understands that we will fail at times. 1 John 1:9 is a verse of comfort, as it provides for a way back to right relationship with Christ when we sin.

If we confess our sins, he is faithful and just to forgive us our sins and to cleanse us from all unrighteousness. —1 John 1:9

RUNNING THE RACE

In the 1992 Olympics in Barcelona, Spain, Derek Redmond, a British runner, was favored to win the 400-meter race. Midway though the race Redmond tore his hamstring and collapsed to the ground. As he struggled to limp his way to the finish line, his father pushed his way onto the field. With assistance from his father, Redmond managed to complete the race, as the crowd rose to their feet, giving him a standing ovation.

One video clip of Redmond's race* has the song "You Raise Me Up" by Josh Groban as the sound track. I cannot watch this without tearing up as I see a man who started so strong, had so much going for him, and expected to cross the finish line as the winner, fall to the tarmac in agonizing pain and then get up to finish the race.

The lyrics read,

---

* https://www.youtube.com/watch?v=A9GWhSndmf0.

When I am down, and, oh, my soul, so weary,
When troubles come, and my heart burdened be,
Then, I am still and wait here in the silence
Until you come and sit awhile with me.
You raise me up, so I can stand on mountains,
You raise me up to walk on stormy seas,
I am strong when I am on your shoulders
You raise me up to more than I can be.

Most of us, when we got married, expected to finish strong. For all of us there have been unexpected challenges in the race. Some have been of our own doing; some have been out of our control. For some of us the challenges have seemed rather minor and simply slowed us down. For others they have been more catastrophic and have thrown us facedown on the ground. When our expectations are not met and the challenges are great, it is easy to quit. What I love about the Redmond story is that when he was down, his father broke through all obstacles to come to his aid and help him finish the race. There also was a "cloud of witnesses" in the stands, cheering him on. The application is obvious. Some of us may feel our fathers not only didn't break through the crowds but actually pushed us down. Others of us have earthly fathers or friends who are willing to break through obstacles to come alongside us in times of challenge. We all have a Heavenly Father who is able to break through every obstacle and come lift us up so that we can finish well. We are fortunate to have a heavenly "cloud of witnesses" cheering us on and hopefully, in addition, human cheerleaders on earth. We may not finish as we expected, but we can finish well.

CHAPTER HIGHLIGHTS

► When it comes to marriage and life, we are all in need of mentors.

► We all have "mentors" in life who, though we realize we will never imitate them perfectly, encourage us to grow.

► Jesus is the only perfect mentor we have. He fully realizes we are human and that we will not be perfect in our attempts to love our wife as He loves the Church.

► Christ does not blame us because we have not "arrived," but encourages each of us to take our experiences and grow into one who honors Him and our wife more fully.

► God calls us to excellence, yet knows we will fail at times. We live in the tension of being loved by God where we are, but having Him encourage us to be so much more than we are.

► No matter what our history is, we are only one generation away from creating a different legacy for our family.

► In this race of life we face many challenges. God and His people are there to come alongside us, pick us up, cheer for us, and help us finish the race.

GAME PLAN

○ Continue reading one chapter of the Gospel of Mark each day this week to get a better view of who this Jesus is.

○ Thank God that He understands you. Thank Him that He wants to lighten your load, not add to it.

TALKIN' WITH THE BROTHERS

1. Who have been your mentors when it comes to marriage and life?

2. How have they encouraged you to grow?

3. What does the tension of being called to be holy, yet realizing you can't be on your own, do to you?

4. What are the challenges that have thrown you to the ground, slowed you down, or discouraged you from finishing well?

5. Tell of a time when someone "broke through the crowd" to help you in life's race.

DISCUSSING THE WORD

⁸Finally, brothers, whatever is true, whatever is honorable, whatever is just, whatever is pure, whatever is lovely, whatever is commendable, if there is any excellence, if there is anything worthy of praise, think about these things. ⁹What you have learned and received and heard and seen in me—practice these things, and the God of peace will be with you.

—Philippians 4:8–9

1. If we want the "God of peace" to be with us, what does this passage say to do?

2. How would doing these things affect your life?

3. Name someone you would like to imitate. Who looks up to you as someone to imitate?

3

What Would Jesus Do?

I don't know, I never saw the movie.

When I was in high school, my English teacher, Mrs. Lincoln, required us to read a certain number of books each semester and write a "book report" on each of them. One of the books on our reading list was the voluminous novel *Hawaii*. The movie "Hawaii" (based on the book), just happened to be showing in our town that semester. Many of us felt that buying a ticket for the movie was a better investment than checking the book out of the library and spending countless hours reading. We watched the movie, wrote our reviews, and smugly handed them in on the assigned day. While collecting the reports, Mrs. Lincoln noticed how many of us had written on the book *Hawaii*. She said with a wry smile on her face, "I am pleased to see how many of you have chosen to write your reports on the book *Hawaii* this week rather than choosing other books that were not as lengthy. I don't know if any of you are aware of this, but the movie 'Hawaii' is actually playing at the Porterville Theater this week. I don't want to spoil the movie for those of you who have yet to see it, but I am sure those of you who have written your reports on the book *Hawaii* will be struck by how significantly different the plot and characters are from the book."

Busted!!

Many of us may have an idea of who Jesus is, but we have never "read the book" to actually know who Jesus is. Or, we may have created a Jesus who meets our own lifestyle or desires.

We were at Fenway Park in Boston watching the Red Sox, who were trailing by two runs in the bottom of the 7th with two on base and two out. The Fenway crowd went wild as the Red Sox center fielder, Johnny Damien, came to the plate. The fans had high hopes that this long-haired Jesus look-alike (as some thought) would hit one out of the park. All of a sudden, from behind us, a rather intoxicated fan screamed, "Johnny, what would Jesus do?" Although the fan had uttered the word "Jesus" many times during the previous innings, I was quite sure this man did not know Jesus personally, let alone know what Jesus "would do."

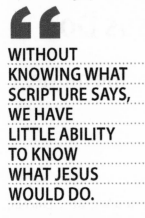

WITHOUT KNOWING WHAT SCRIPTURE SAYS, WE HAVE LITTLE ABILITY TO KNOW WHAT JESUS WOULD DO.

I often remember that incident when I think of the challenge the apostle Paul gives husbands in Ephesians 5 to love their wives *"as Christ loved the church."* What would Jesus do? What sort of a husband would Jesus be? What does it really mean, practically, for me to love my wife the way Jesus would?

What does "Jesus-like" love look like? How do we even start trying to love like Christ? I know a Christian man who led a young woman to Christ and then led her into the bedroom to have sex. She was a bit perplexed and asked if sex before marriage was acceptable in the Christian faith. He assured her it was, because it was "loving"—and Jesus instructed us to love. But the advice this "Christian" gave to the new convert had more to do with his genitals than his genuine faith.

Too often we let the world's concept of "love"—or our own selfish desires—rule over us, rather than letting scripture guide our thinking through the example of Christ.

Many of us give it our best shot, but instead of loving our wives the way Christ would, we tend to love them the way we would like to be loved. Without a thorough knowledge of how Jesus loved the Church, we will have little idea of the meaning of love, let alone how we are to love our wives.

Some years ago it was popular for Christians to wear bracelets bearing the letters WWJD, meaning "What Would Jesus Do?" I applaud the desire to do what Jesus would do, but without a knowledge of scripture it is difficult to know what that would be. I believe a better bracelet would bear the letters WDSS, for "What Does Scripture Say?" Without knowing what scripture says, we have little ability to know what Jesus would do. We need to love our wives, not as we would like to be loved, not as the popular media say we should love them, not even as our parents modeled love, but as Christ did Himself.

WILL IMITATING CHRIST MAKE ME A WUSS?

If we are honest, some of us believe that loving our wives like Christ means we have to spend our mornings eating quiche, our afternoons shopping, and our evenings watching chick flicks. We often see Jesus as a bit effeminate and are afraid that following Him will require giving up our masculinity, and that we will end up being "sweet and nice." Perhaps for some of us, the real issue is that we're not sure we *want* to be like Christ. Our view of Him has been someone who is sweet, weak, not popular, and certainly not fun. We are afraid that if we are like Jesus we will never get to do what we want. So let's take a few pages and look at this man we are being called to imitate.

- **He was a man's man.**

The guys He hung around with—His posse, if you will—were not quite the effeminate-looking intellectuals of the day that might be depicted in some of our Bible story books. First, He called some fishermen to follow Him. These were not your "tie your own flies"-type guys who stand in a river all day in their waders. These were rugged men who hauled boats up onto the beach and dragged in huge nets and large catches of fish. He also called Matthew, who was a tax collector—not the kind who sits at a computer, but the Mafia-type that squeezes it out of you. He gave James and John the nickname "Sons of Thunder." I don't know exactly what He meant by that, but it does not seem to describe men who would be nominated for choirboys of the year. When people opposed Jesus, these two had an idea of how to handle it:

When the disciples James and John saw this, they asked, "Lord, do you want us to call fire down from heaven to destroy them?"

—Luke 9:54 (NIV)

That's one way to get rid of the opposition. What I am saying here is that Jesus was a man's man. He had to be, to lead this group of rough and tough men.

JESUS IS ANYTHING BUT "SAFE"— BUT HE IS GOOD.

Some people are afraid that if they "love like Jesus" they will become someone with a totally different personality, or drive, or sense of humor. One of my favorite characters in the Bible is Peter. Peter was a man of passion and impulse. If he were living today, we might say he had a bit of an "impulse control issue." His communication often seemed to be without a filter. He was the one who said that even if all the disciples denied the Lord, he would not—and then, soon after, he denied he ever knew Jesus . . . three times! When Jesus was about to be arrested, Peter is the one who drew his sword and cut off the ear of one of the guards. The guard lost only his ear only because Peter was a bit off on his aim and missed decapitating him. Peter was the one who jumped out of the boat to walk on the water towards Jesus and then sank—but he was the only one who jumped in the water and walked at all. I think Jesus loved the passion and life in Peter. He was one of Jesus' closest friends, and God later used him in amazing ways to build a community of followers of Christ—not because he had become "sweet," but because God used him as he was created to be. Peter was a leader, and Jesus used his God-given temperament to further His purposes. I believe He will use your God-given temperament for His purposes as well.

Are you the life of the party? He wants to make you even more so, for His glory. Are you impulsive? You still will be, but hopefully to further His Kingdom. Are you an introvert? Use those traits to think deeply about issues.

- **He was a passionate man.**

When Jesus entered the city of Jerusalem, He saw people using the temple as a marketplace, selling animals and birds. He didn't gently whisper, "Excuse me, would you mind leaving? This is actually my Father's house, and He will be really sad if He finds out you are doing this." The scriptures record the interaction differently:

> *And making a whip of cords, he drove them all out of the temple, with the sheep and oxen. And he poured out the coins of the money-changers and overturned their tables. And he told those who sold the pigeons, "Take these things away; do not make my Father's house a house of trade." His disciples remembered that it was written, "Zeal for your house will consume me."* —John 2:15–17

Don't miss this: *"And making a whip of cords, he drove them all out of the temple."* Jesus was ticked. He saw what was happening, went away, made a whip, and then came back and used it!

In C. S. Lewis's *The Lion, the Witch, and the Wardrobe*, Susan and Lucy are talking to Mrs. Beaver about Aslan, the Lion (who is a representation of Christ):

> "Don't you know who is the King of Beasts? Aslan is a lion—the Lion, the great Lion."
>
> "Ooh!" said Susan. "I'd thought he was a man. Is he—quite safe? I shall feel rather nervous about meeting a lion."
>
> "That you will, dearie, and no mistake," said Mrs. Beaver; "if there's anyone who can appear before Aslan without their knees knocking, they're either braver than most or else just silly."
>
> "Then he isn't safe?" said Lucy.
>
> "Safe?" said Mr. Beaver; "don't you hear what Mrs. Beaver tells you? Who said anything about safe? Of course he isn't safe. But he is good."

Jesus is anything but "safe"—but He is good.

- **He was a compassionate man.**

In John 8, when the scribes and the Pharisees brought to Jesus a woman who had been caught in adultery and said she should be stoned, I guess they forgot it takes two to commit adultery. Jesus silenced the crowd as He stood and said to them,

> *"Let him who is without sin among you be the first to throw a stone at her." And once more he bent down and wrote on the ground. But when they heard it, they went away one by one, beginning with the older ones, and Jesus was left alone with the woman standing before him. Jesus stood up and said to her, "Woman, where are they? Has no one condemned you?" She said, "No one, Lord." And Jesus said, "Neither do I condemn you; go, and from now on sin no more."*
>
> *—John 8:7–11*

Scripture does not record what Jesus wrote on the ground, but given the men's response, I wonder if it was something very simple, such as "Joseph: drunkenness," "José: infidelity," "George: anger," "Andrew: lust." I am glad I was not in that circle of men.

Scripture elsewhere shows how Jesus cared deeply for the marginalized, children, women, the poor, and those in need of healing. He was a compassionate man.

- **He was an outspoken man.**

He came to heal the lost, but He blasted the self-righteous.

He is, what we call in counseling, one who uses the direct method. He was not politically correct or afraid of offending. As one of my favorite comedians, Brian Regan, says, "I don't want to step on anyone's toes, but, here we go . . ."

> *"Woe to you, scribes and Pharisees, hypocrites! For you are like whitewashed tombs, which outwardly appear beautiful, but within are full of dead people's bones and all uncleanness."*
>
> *—Matthew 23:27*

He was intolerant of self-righteous, holier-than-thou, duplicitous religious folk.

- **He was a humorous man.**

Yes, Jesus was funny. When I was a youth, just before TV was invented, we told elephant jokes. Elephant jokes were basically absurdities, such as,

> How do you tell an elephant from a grape?
> Answer: The grape is purple.

> How can you tell if an elephant has been in your refrigerator?
> Answer: By the footprints on the pizza box.

Okay, so maybe it was just a thing for young boys in the 1950s, but don't miss the point. In Luke 6:39–42, Jesus is in essence telling "elephant jokes"—absurdities. As you read this passage, picture a talented cartoonist drawing the images:

> *"Can a blind man lead a blind man? Will they not both fall into a pit? A disciple is not above his teacher, but everyone when he is fully trained will be like his teacher. Why do you see the speck that is in your brother's eye, but do not notice the log that is in your own eye? How can you say to your brother, 'Brother, let me take out the speck that is in your eye,' when you yourself do not see the log that is in your own eye? You hypocrite, first take the log out of your own eye, and then you will see clearly to take out the speck that is in your brother's eye.*
> —Luke 6:39–42

I think people were chuckling as the Rabbi painted these pictures with words, absurd things that just should not happen. Then, He tells His final "joke," the greatest absurdity:

> *"Why do you call me 'Lord, Lord,' and not do what I tell you?"*
> —Luke 6:46

They likely stopped laughing then. But he used humor to "set the stage." It's okay to be funny, to laugh, and to have a good time. After all, we are called to imitate the One who came to give us *"life to the full"* (John 10:10, NIV).

49

- **He was an intriguing man.**

Wherever Jesus went, a crowd followed. Jesus was intriguing and people kept following Him wherever He went.

And great crowds followed him from Galilee and the Decapolis, and from Jerusalem and Judea, and from beyond the Jordan.
—Matthew 4:25

When he came down from the mountain, great crowds followed him. *—Matthew 8:1*

Now when Jesus heard this, he withdrew from there in a boat to a desolate place by himself. But when the crowds heard it, they followed him on foot from the towns. *—Matthew 14:13*

And when they could not get near him because of the crowd, they removed the roof above him, and when they had made an opening, they let down the bed on which the paralytic lay. *—Mark 2:4*

But too many times, Christians are viewed as irritating rather than intriguing. Maybe it's because we sometimes forget that the Good News actually is good news. When we live out our lives in life-giving ways, people should be intrigued to hear more about this man Jesus.

I officiated at a wedding for a nationally-known family a number of years ago. After the ceremony, the uncle of the groom came up to me and said, "Pastor, I was intrigued by your message. I have never heard a talk on marriage like that, and I have been married six times."

And it was at Wes Welker's wedding that a well-known Hollywood writer and actor came up to me, introduced himself, and said, "That was really good! I mean, I don't know if everyone caught all the humor, but I did. That is really good stuff. Where do you get your material?" I wanted to say, "From God," but I thought it would sound a bit like name-dropping.

- **He was not a dull man.**

People don't follow boring, dull people. But wherever Jesus went, people were healed, pigs ran off cliffs, demons were cast out, multitudes were fed with one boy's lunch, people walked on water. Are you afraid that imitating Jesus will lead to a boring life? I love the slogan

I saw over the entrance to a trapeze school: "Forget fear. Worry about the addiction." Don't be afraid of what following Christ more fully will do to you; worry about the addiction you will develop as you learn what God wants to do with your life. *So*, buckle up as we look at the book that tells His story—and yours.

ANY GOOD BOOKS?

Ray Johnston, pastor of Bayside Church in Granite Bay, California, tells the story of a man who made a decision to follow Christ. He was counseled and given his first Bible and encouraged to go home and start reading it. He came back the next Sunday and found Ray. "Hey, I loved that book you gave me last week. Has God written anything else?"

Actually, all we need to know about Jesus is written in the scriptures, but we often spend more time listening to sports radio or reading the morning news than reading the scriptures. I mention this not to increase guilt, but hopefully to increase interest.

Just as many of us have a less-than-accurate picture of who Jesus is, we also often fail to realize what an exciting book the Bible is. This may be because we have preconceived misconceptions about the Bible, believing that it is boring, just a bunch of burdensome rules, or not practical.

BURDENSOME?

Many years ago when all our girls were young, Virginia and I got away for an overnight at a hotel in Southern California that had an outdoor pool. Our oldest daughter, Kari (age 5), was just learning to swim and wanted me to see her accomplishments. Virginia was nursing our youngest daughter, Julie, while Lisa (age 3) was playing near the pool. I told Lisa to stay away from the pool while I watched Kari. Kari was doing a great job showing Daddy her best dog paddle and was making progress across the pool when someone from the balcony of the hotel started screaming. I couldn't make out what they were saying, but I was a bit annoyed that they were interrupting this special time—until I finally made out one word, "drowning," and immediately looked around to see Lisa in the pool, treading water, six inches under the surface. My annoyance turned to profound gratitude to the one who had a vantage point that I did not and was willing to share her knowledge. How many times have I felt God's Word was interrupting something when in fact He saw and communicated through His Word what I did not see, and saved me from "drowning." Scripture says it well:

> *For this is the love of God, that we keep his commandments. And his commandments are not burdensome.*   —1 John 5:3

Whether or not you have a relationship with Christ or even believe in the Bible, I hope you will be willing to see what practical and helpful insights it has that allow us to experience even more than we ever hoped or imagined in marriage.

CHAPTER HIGHLIGHTS

▶ Often our views about Jesus come from what we have heard or imagined rather than by actually reading the accounts of His life.

▶ We often let our personal preferences, or our hormones, define love for our wives instead of listening to God's Word.

▶ When you read about Jesus, you will find that:
   1. He was a man's man.
   2. He was a passionate man.
   3. He was a compassionate man.
   4. He was a humorous man.
   5. He was an intriguing man.
   6. He was not a dull man.

▶ All the principles we need to know about God, love, and marriage are found in the Bible.

▶ Knowing God's Word and following it is not a burden, but actually life-giving.

GAME PLAN

o   Continue reading one chapter a day of Mark, noting anything you discover about who Jesus is.

TALKIN' WITH THE BROTHERS

1. Where did you get your view of Jesus as you grew up?

2. What did you think a follower of Jesus would be like?

3. What struck you about the descriptions of Jesus in this chapter?
   - He was a man's man.
   - He was a passionate man.
   - He was a compassionate man.
   - He was a humorous man.
   - He was an intriguing man.
   - He was not a dull man.

4. What do you feel most hinders men from reading the Bible more?

5. What challenges you personally in your pursuit of Christ?

6. Name a man you feel lives out some of the characteristics used to describe Jesus in this chapter.

7. How do you think being a more fully devoted follower of Christ might affect your relationship with your wife?

DISCUSSING THE WORD

²Early in the morning he came again to the temple. All the people came to him, and he sat down and taught them. ³The scribes and the Pharisees brought a woman who had been caught in adultery, and placing her in the midst ⁴they said to him, "Teacher, this woman has been caught in the act of adultery. ⁵Now in the Law, Moses commanded us to stone such women. So what do you say?" ⁶This they said to test him, that they might have some charge to bring against him. Jesus bent down and wrote with his finger on the ground. ⁷And as they continued to ask him, he stood up and said to them, "Let him who is without sin among you be the first to throw a stone at her." ⁸And once more he bent down and wrote on the ground. ⁹But when they heard it, they went away one by one, beginning with the older ones, and Jesus was left alone with the woman standing before him. ¹⁰Jesus stood up and said to her, "Woman, where are they? Has no one condemned you?" ¹¹She said, "No one, Lord." And Jesus said, "Neither do I condemn you; go, and from now on sin no more." —John 8:2–11

1. In what situations might we act like the scribes and Pharisees?

2. What do you think Jesus was writing on the ground?

3. What strikes you about the interaction between Jesus and the woman?

4

Jesus Understood the Church

But have you met my wife?

A friend of mine, a doctor, wanted to get the perfect Valentine gift for his wife. He asked the nurses he worked with what he should purchase. Perfume, candy, and flowers were suggested, but the number one recommendation was a sexy negligee. He went to the mall and, with much embarrassment, entered a store he had never ventured into before. When a clerk asked how she could help him, it took all he had to get out, "I want to buy my wife a sexy red negligee." After some awkward and humorous exchanges about size, he headed home with wrapped box in hand. His very reserved and private wife opened her Valentine gift with excitement. However, as soon as she opened the box, embarrassment turned her face close to the color of the nightie. Their teenage daughters were shocked that dad would buy such a gift, and it sits to this day in a closet, collecting dust rather than the memories he had hoped for. He learned that day that he did not know his wife as well as he imagined and that every wife does not wish for the same thing.

One of the most discouraging comments Virginia can make to me, after 42 years of marriage, is: "Don't you even know me?"

Most of us men don't naturally "get" women. Men and women are really different. On the second day of our honeymoon, Virginia and I were driving up Highway 1 in the Big Sur area of California. A squirrel ran in front of our car and we both looked back to see what had happened. At the exact same time, Virginia put her head in her hands and sighed, "Ohhhh," while I shouted triumphantly, *"Got it!"* We are *so* different. That was just the first of many differences we have discovered in the way we act and think.

In Genesis, after God pronounced it was not good for Adam to be alone, He said he would make a helper fit for him—written *"ēzer k'negdǒ,"* in the Hebrew, which literally means "like" him, but "like opposite" him. * Eve was "like" him in that she was the only other creature made in the image of God as Adam was. She was equal to Adam in every way, yet not the same. But she was "like opposite" in that she was very different from Adam. Her body was different, her mind thought differently, and she related differently. Because women were intentionally created as different from us men, it is not surprising that we have difficulty understanding them. Perhaps this is why Peter challenges men to live with their wives in an understanding way. It does not come naturally to us.

> *. . . husbands, live with your wives in an understanding way . . .*
> —1 Peter 3:7

One mistake we often make, however, is that, supposing we will never understand the mind of a woman, we give up trying to enter her world.

IF I LIKE IT, SHE SHOULD LIKE IT

One of the mistakes we make in understanding our wives is thinking our likes will be her likes. We really do need to be students of our wives if we are going to learn to understand and love them well. Our good friends Ryan and Kelly Plosker tell of how this way of thinking played out in the early years of their marriage. On Ryan's birthday, he would waken to a beautifully wrapped gift from Kelly. As the day wore on, other gifts would follow. Late in the afternoon the "big gift" of the day would be given—usually an item of clothing. Ryan would

---

*Wenham, Gordon. *Genesis 1–15* (Word Biblical Commentary), Nashville, TN: Nelson, 1987, p. 68

thank Kelly and then say something like, "Where are we going for my birthday dinner?" to which she would reply, "You're wearing it." On Kelly's birthday, Ryan would give her an invitation for a date and ask her to be ready to leave the house at 6:30 pm. As they finished their incredible steak dinner, Kelly would ask, "Do you have any presents for me?" to which Ryan would reply, "You just ate them." Both well-meaning spouses were operating on the premise, "If I like it, my spouse should like it." Part of our task as husbands is to become familiar with what *she* likes and do that.

WALKIN' IN HER HIGH HEELS

If we are going to love our wives as Christ loved the Church, we had better look at how Christ interacted with the Church.

Jesus loved the Church by living among its members and experiencing their joys, sorrows, strengths, weaknesses, temptations, triumphs, and failures. The first chapter of the gospel of John tells us that *"The Word [Jesus] became flesh and made His dwelling among us."* (John 1:14). Or, literally, "built his tent among us"—He lived in our world.

One of the most well-known verses in the Bible is John 3:16, which tells us of the enormous sacrifice God made. He didn't send us an email or a text—He sent His only Son to live on earth with us:

"For God so loved the world, that he gave his only Son, that whoever believes in him should not perish but have eternal life." —John 3:16

Jesus was born as a human baby. He entered our world! He grew up as a normal child. He experienced the joys and trials of adolescence. The Bible says that Jesus *"increased in wisdom and in stature and in favor with God and man"* (Luke 2:52). Although the full implication of this verse is unclear, it implies He was "in process" and that He knew what that felt like. He experienced the temptations of young adulthood and difficult choices as an adult. He fished with the fishermen, worked as a carpenter, went to the synagogue, talked in the temple, listened to women's concerns. He truly lived among us. In addition, He was accused of being a glutton and a drunkard by some, and of being blasphemous by others. He experienced misunderstanding, rejection, betrayal, and desertion.

Referring to Jesus, the book of Hebrews states:

For we do not have a high priest who is unable to sympathize with our weaknesses, but one who in every respect has been tempted as we are, yet without sin. —Hebrews 4:15

It would have been "easier" for Him to observe us from afar, but he lived among us and can truly say, "I know what you are going through."

The apostle Peter instructs us to:

. . . live with your wives in an understanding way, showing honor to the woman as the weaker vessel, since they are heirs with you of the grace of life, so that your prayers may not be hindered.

—1 Peter 3:7

"Weaker" certainly does not imply inferiority or lacking strength, but it does imply someone who is more delicate, fragile, or valuable. For instance, there are drinking glasses in our house that I don't wash, because they are delicate, fragile, and valuable—and I am *not* delicate, shall we say. There are clothes of Virginia's I don't wash because they are valuable and need to be handled with special care.

Men don't naturally "think like a woman" and never will, but we do need to work to more fully understand them. We just think differently. If Virginia says to me, "Those pants seem a bit tight; have you gained weight?" I'll respond, "Not that I know of. Could you pass the French fries and catsup, please?" But if I say to her, "Those pants seem a bit tight; have you gained weight?" I won't see her naked that night. We are just different.

This is so important to God that the 1 Peter scripture referenced above actually says that when we don't honor our wives as valuable and equal, our prayers are hindered. Too often we as husbands have little knowledge of our wives, let alone appreciation for who they are and what they do.

AFFIRM HER

I remember like it was yesterday the counseling session where a husband said in front of his wife, "I mean, raising our three young children is at best a half-time job. Why do I have to work full-time while she is at home doing nothing?" She was devastated by his lack of understanding of her day.

When our girls were 10, 8, and 6, Virginia had a dear friend who invited her to accompany her on an 18-day trip to Europe, all expenses paid. Believing I would never have enough money to send her to Europe, I said, "Sure, go! I'll work out of the house and watch the children. How hard can that be?" I distinctly remember one morning trying to put Lisa's hair up in pigtails when she sweetly said, "Mommy usually has them more even." One day, Julie would not cooperate with her hair being brushed at all, so I gave her a brush and some hair bands and said "Have your teacher do it." At the end of the 18 days I was more than happy to "turn in my high heels." My understanding of Virginia's world had grown immensely. You can bet that upon her return, I lavished her with praise for all she did, day in and day out.

I'm also reminded of the story of the husband who frequently asked his wife what she did all day. One evening he arrived home from work to find her still in her bathrobe, curlers in her hair, the house a mess, dinner not made, and the kids totally out of control. "What happened?!" he shouted. She looked at him and said, "You know all those times you've asked me what I did all day? Well, today I didn't do it." Enough said!

A couple came to see Virginia and me for counseling. We opened our session with the question we use at almost every first session with new clients. "Why are we here today?" The wife started and was going on in some detail about their history and the events she felt contributed to the issue at hand. After listening for a short time, her husband turned to her and said, "For heaven's sake, can't you just net it out?" She ended her story and was silent the rest of the session.

Compare this to the story in the Bible of the woman with the issue of blood who touched the robe of Jesus and was healed. The Biblical account says the woman had this issue for 12 years and told Jesus all about it. Jesus did not say, "Net it out, woman. You are healed, aren't you? What else do you want?" Jesus took time and listened to the woman's whole medical history, because it was important to her, and He showed His respect and love for her. Are we husbands willing to listen to the whole story from our wives, with interest? We listen not because we need to hear every detail, but because it is important for us to hear what she wants to share.

But he went on asking, looking around to see who had done it. The woman, knowing what had happened, knowing she was the one, stepped up in fear and trembling, knelt before him, and gave him the whole story.   *—Mark 5:33 (MSG)*

It is easy for us to miss the hearts of our wives because we become impatient. We often fail to give our wives our full attention as they speak in more detail than we wish. For our wives, connection through conversation is critically important. The analogous situation for husbands might be when starting to make love, your wife says to you, "For heaven's sake, can you hurry up and get this over with?"

ASK ABOUT HER DAY

We will never be able to fully understand our wives, but for starters, we can at least ask our wives about their lives, their day, their joys, and their concerns.

I recently came across a cartoon with a wife speaking to her husband. "If you want to know how to make me happy, just ask. You don't have to look everything up on the Internet!"

Part of entering her world is asking follow-up questions that show you were actually listening to her first response. We often want our wives to answer us like we answer them when they ask us how our day was: "Fine." But usually they will have more than a monosyllabic response. If we are wise, we will listen closely (this often will involve putting down the newspaper or cell phone, or turning off the TV). Wives need us to focus on them and give them our full attention. It means showing appreciation for what she is doing and has done. Many of us have a lot to learn about showing appreciation to our wives. Too often our humor belittles them or makes light of their work. If your wife is a stay-at-home mom caring for children, she is working full time. I am convinced the reason many women re-enter the marketplace is to find an environment in which they are appreciated and affirmed. I am also convinced there is no harder job or any job more important than influencing the next generation for Christ. Let's make sure our wives know how thankful we are for them.

The word that keeps jumping out at me is "initiative." Our wives long for us to take initiative to ask them about their day, ask them out, or ask what they would like to do this year for vacation. My experience is they don't need us to have all the answers, but they do need us to take more of an interest in them.

WE LISTEN NOT BECAUSE WE NEED TO HEAR EVERY DETAIL, BUT BECAUSE IT IS IMPORTANT FOR US TO HEAR WHAT SHE WANTS TO SHARE.

Recently Virginia and I met with a couple where the wife did not feel her husband took enough of an interest in her. He described to us all the work he did around the house to help out, and she affirmed this was true—but she said it felt more like a business arrangement of duties than a marriage in which she was sincerely being cared for. She then went on to give an example of a time she felt truly cared for. She said, "Since my teenage years, I always have severe abdominal pain during my monthly cycle. After being married for 16 years, one Sunday morning on our way to church in the car my husband reached over to touch my hand and asked very gently, 'How are you feeling? Does it hurt?' I was so shocked and so happy for the rest of the day. He filled up my emotional tank with that simple gesture, expressing that he thought of me and that I mattered to him."

Our wives wish to be understood and to know of our interest in their lives. Many times we fail to express what we feel for them. A simple gesture like a touch on the arm or a question about their day goes a long way in helping them feel our love for them.

A WORD FROM THE WIVES

We have surveyed wives and will include some of their responses at the end of each chapter from here on out. The thing that struck me most about their answers is that wives really are not looking for that much. They want their husbands to show interest in them, take initiative, and care for them.

Here were their answers when asked to complete the question **"I feel most understood by my husband when . . ."**

- "He does something to take care of me without being asked. It could be something very incidental (picking up my favorite treat on the way home) or something of great significance. Either way, knowing he is romancing me this way hits a deep spot."

- "He sees something that I need before I tell him I need it, such as doing the dishes before I ask, or helping me with the kids when he can tell things are crazy."

- "He listens to me without looking at his iPad or the TV while I'm talking."

- "He listens to me without distractions (phone, computer, time restraints, chores) and really listens!"

- "He gives me his time and attention."

- "He says, 'Yeah, I understand' like he means it."

- "He takes the time to listen to my day, my thoughts, my fears, even just mundane, everyday things. I also love it when he 'has my back' when I come home frustrated or hurt by something or someone."

- "He stops for me and gives me his undivided attention to listen, not to lecture or instruct. I feel understood when he shows me later that he was listening—by remembering what it was that was important at that moment of time."

- "He looks me in my eyes and says 'I love you' and 'I am so glad you are in my life.' When he listens to me with his heart."

And a couple of "not understood" responses:

- "I don't feel understood. Actually, I very rarely ever felt I was understood."
- "One time I was really upset about a trip I had to take with our newborn son on an airplane. It was exhausting and difficult, and when I was talking to him about it, tears streaming down my face, recalling how hard it was to be alone with the baby in a hotel, he just sat there stoic as could be—not even once offering an 'I'm sorry' or 'That sounds so hard' or patting my shoulder. I had no idea if he was listening to me at all! Needless to say, I was not only sad and frustrated about my trip, I was getting very angry with him for seemingly not caring at all at how upset I was!"

CHAPTER HIGHLIGHTS

▶ Being created as male and female literally means "like, but like opposite," so it should come as no surprise that we don't naturally "get" one another.

▶ Jesus came from heaven and lived with us. I think we have a hard time understanding what a deep sacrifice that was.

▶ We need to put ourselves as much as possible in our wives' "high heels" to understand their worlds.

▶ It is important to ask how their day has been, and then actually listen to the answer.

▶ We need to express appreciation for what they do.

▶ Our wives are more fragile and need more gentle care than we might naturally give to a guy.

▶ Taking initiative with our wives is critical.

GAME PLAN

Here are some suggestions for things to say or do for your wife. Don't go crazy—just pick a few.

o "How was your day today?"

o "What can I do to help you with dinner?"

o "Sounds like you've had a very full day. Could I watch the children so you can take a walk (or a bath)?"

o "Sounds like you've had a rough day. Let's go out to dinner."

o "Thanks so much for being such a great mom. Our kids are very fortunate to have you as a mom."

o After dinner, get up and do the dishes without asking if she needs help.

o Before you leave for work in the morning, ask your wife what's on her schedule for the day. Ask if there is anything you can do to lighten her load and then pray for her before you leave. This doesn't need to be a 20-minute prayer. It can be a 20-second prayer, bringing her needs to the Lord before you run out the door.

o Tell your wife you are taking a day off work to watch the children so she can do some things she has wanted or needed to do.

o Suggest to your wife that she go away for the weekend with some friends or by herself—whichever is more refreshing—and you'll watch the children (without your mom's help!).

o While she is out at a meeting or out shopping, clean an area of the house, do laundry, or do something that will show her you understand some of her workload and would like to lessen it.

TALKIN' WITH THE BROTHERS

1. In what areas does it tend to be the hardest to understand your wife?

2. How would you describe the depth of Jesus' sacrifice in becoming a man and living among us?

3. What are some of the ways you feel you have been successful in learning to understand your wife more fully?

4. What is one thing you could implement from this chapter that would help your wife feel more understood this week?

DISCUSSING THE WORD

⁷Likewise, husbands, live with your wives in an understanding way, showing honor to the woman as the weaker vessel, since they are heirs with you of the grace of life, so that your prayers may not be hindered.

—1 Peter 3:7

1. Of all the things the apostle Peter could have said, why does he tell us to "live with your wives in an understanding way"?

2. What truths does this passage tell us about our wives?

3. How could the way you treat your wife affect your prayers?

5

Jesus Pursued the Church

I pursued my wife once, too.

"I told you I loved you 40 years ago when we were married, and if anything changes, I'll let you know."

That might be good for a laugh, but it's not good if you want your marriage to flourish. I don't know a lot about women, but one thing I do know from 42 years of marriage and countless counseling sessions: women want to be chosen and pursued.

Years ago, each of us pursued the woman we wanted to win. I remember like yesterday my first date with Virginia. That was over 44 years ago, so I am sure my rendition of it now is better than it actually was. I sent Virginia a typed letter (those of you who are under 40, Google "typewriters" to learn what I am referring to). I invited her to accompany me to dinner at a fine location, with wonderful company and great food. I wanted to surprise her, so I asked if I could blindfold her. I would never allow my daughters say yes to such an invitation, but Virginia did say yes. To cut to the chase, I drove her to Sunset Cliffs overlooking the Pacific Ocean in San Diego. When she opened her eyes, there was a table for two set with candles and a complete meal from salad to dessert that I had made. The Carpenters were crooning "We've only just begun . . ." on my cassette tape player (you can Google that as well).

Okay, perhaps I should not have started our dating relationship with my "best date" idea, but I wanted this woman! We were married two and a half years later. Fast forward to a more recent celebration, her birthday. I rolled over in bed when the alarm went off, and there on my nightstand were a few "Wife's Birthday" cards she had purchased (on sale) for me to select from and give to her. Where had the creativity, pursuit, and romance gone?

Back when we were pursuing the women who are now our wives, we often went out to eat at places we couldn't afford, watched movies we thought we would never watch, bought flowers we knew would die, drove cars that we had borrowed, and acted interested in conversations with her when we had no clue what she was talking about. My point is not that we should fake who we are; it is that we can and should be more intentional about pursuing the woman we are married to.

FIGHTING FOR HER, NOT AGAINST HER

In his wonderful book *Wild at Heart*, John Eldredge talks about every young girl's dream of being the princess rescued by the knight in shining armor.

> Every woman needs to know that she is exquisite and exotic and *chosen*. This is core to her identity, the way she bears the image of God. *Will you pursue me? Do you delight in me? Will you fight for me?*
> —John Eldredge, *Wild at Heart*, p. 182

I was counseling a man whose wife was involved with another man. As we talked, he told me that his wife said the other man treated her well, took her places, and was interested in her. I asked the man what he was going to do. "Well, I love her so much, all I want is for her to be happy, and if she is happier with this other man than with me, I guess I will just support her choice and try to help our children deal with this new arrangement." *Are you kidding me?* If you love her and your children, you will fight for her and pursue her. Confess where you have fallen short and be the man who won her over 10 years ago. Call up her new "boyfriend" and tell him to bug off, that the woman he is involved with is your wife and the mother of your children. Help him know in no uncertain terms you are not going to just sit back and allow him to ruin your marriage and family. As for your wife, the grass will always look greener on the other side of the fence unless you start watering your own grass (the kind you cut, not the kind you smoke).

PURSUED AND CHOSEN

Virginia and I were sitting with a couple that had been married for 30 years and were now contemplating divorce. As we listened to their history, we learned that they had become pregnant early in their dating relationship and felt they "had" to get married for the sake of their families and their own reputation, so a wedding was soon on the calendar. After they finished their story, we turned to the woman and asked her, "Have you ever felt chosen? Do you think your husband would have chosen to marry you if the pregnancy had not occurred?" She immediately burst into tears, "I have always wondered if he would have married me. I have never been courted, chosen, or really pursued by him, since we had to get married."

> **EVERY WOMAN NEEDS TO KNOW THAT SHE IS EXQUISITE AND EXOTIC AND *CHOSEN*.**

Some of our stories are not as dramatic, but many of our wives are wondering, "Would he marry me again if he had the choice?" One of our roles as pursuing husbands is to assure our wives through words and actions that we love them and will continue to pursue them as long as we live.

It is really not that hard to say "I love you." But don't pursue her during the day just so she'll respond in bed at night. Your role is to love your wife in a Christ-like manner, regardless of her response.

For many men, there are four or five days they dread more than any others: her birthday, your anniversary, Christmas, Valentine's Day, and if you have children, Mother's Day. The chances of us getting it right are about the same as winning the lottery—okay, so winning the lottery has a bit of an edge. As much as you might be tempted to quit when she lets you know you didn't get it right, don't quit! Find out how you might better hit the mark. One of my mentors creatively cares for his wife by carrying a card in his wallet with his wife's blouse size, pants size, dress size, favorite flowers, favorite coffee, favorite ice cream, favorite chocolate—you get the idea. Now, when he is out and he sees flowers, he simply looks at his card and asks, "How much are the stargazer lilies?"

JESUS' EXAMPLE OF PURSUIT

Jesus is relentless in continuing to pursue His bride, the Church. Jesus stands at the door and knocks:

> *"Behold, I stand at the door and knock. If anyone hears my voice and opens the door, I will come in to him and eat with him, and he with me."* —Revelation 3:20

He tries to woo His bride:

> *He came to his own, and his own people did not receive him.* —John 1:11

He wants to care for His bride:

> *"O Jerusalem, Jerusalem, the city that kills the prophets and stones those who are sent to it! How often would I have gathered your children together as a hen gathers her brood under her wings, and you were not willing!"* —Matthew 23:37

Jesus continued to pursue relationships with His Church. When Zacchaeus accepted Christ, Jesus didn't keep on truckin', but ate with him and spent the night. He challenges His disciples not only to preach the Gospel and to baptize, but also to make disciples, that is, to form ongoing relationships.

In the classic booklet *My Heart, Christ's Home*, Robert Munger portrays accepting Christ into our life as inviting Him to come live in our home with us. At one point, when the homeowner has missed spending time in the library with Christ, Christ says, "What you may not understand is that I desire to spend time with you." What an incredible truth: The Creator of the Universe wants to spend time with me!

If the Lord of Lord and King of Kings pursues us to spend time with us, and we are called to imitate Him, how can we not be more intentional about spending time pursuing our mate?

One of the most frequent reasons given by couples for coming to see us for marriage counseling is they "no longer love each other." What they often mean is they no longer have the emotional excitement for each other that they once had. We often ask them to describe when they "lost that lovin' feelin.'" Occasionally it is a cataclysmic event such as adultery, loss of a job, or the death of a child—but more frequently they look at each other and say, "I don't know, we just gradually have fallen away from each other."

When Virginia and I moved from California to Massachusetts, many New Englanders questioned us as to why anyone would live in California, given the threat of earthquakes. They were shocked when I told them that more houses are destroyed in California by termites than by earthquakes. An earthquake is certainly devastating to a house, but so are termites as they quietly eat away at the infrastructure.

May I suggest that more marriages are destroyed by "marital termites" than by "marital earthquakes." I am not minimizing the effect of catastrophic events to a marriage such as an affair, but for most couples that have simply "lost that lovin' feelin,'" it has happened because of untreated "marital termites" that have eaten away at their once strong marital relationship.

Some great friends of ours attended a Christian college where they had been best friends with nine other couples that had married either their last year of college or their first year after. Our friends told us that 10 years after graduation, all nine of the couples were divorced. "What was it?" we asked. "Infidelity, substance abuse, financial issues?" No, for all nine the cause was the same: dissatisfaction.

Don't ignore "marital termites." Exterminate them before they damage your marriage.

Our house and yard looked better 24 years ago when we first purchased our house than it does today. It looks worse now not because it's older, but because I am not much of a maintainer. Our yard is more overgrown than it was, some of our windows don't work properly, and the back deck has deteriorated because I have not oiled the wood to protect it from the elements. In contrast, there are some older homes in our area that have been well maintained and they show it.

There are areas of our marriage that were in better shape 42 years ago as well. Many of us put more effort into taking care of our yards, houses, cars, golf equipment, or guns than we do our marriages. Yet, for those of us who take care of our marriages, they truly do have the potential to be more beautiful today than on the day we said "I do."

YOU WON'T WANT A NEW WIFE, YOU'LL HAVE ONE

He was 30 years old, yet he was sobbing like a baby. "My dad just called to tell me he left my mom for another woman. Dad said when he takes his mistress out to restaurants they laugh and engage the whole time, that the little vacations they take are magical, that she loves the gifts he gives her, that the time they spend together talking is energizing—and the sex is 'like I was 20 again.'" When his dad finished his soliloquy on the delights of being with his mistress, the son shot back at his dad. "When did you last go on a vacation with mom, just sit and talk, give her a thoughtful gift, go to a romantic restaurant, or care for her sexual needs? If you had ever done half the things you have done with and for your mistress for mom, do you think the two of you would be where you are today?"

Our wives want us to continue to pursue and choose them.

When our ministry sponsors a marriage conference, we often end with a song by Christian recording artist Danny Oertli*, "Marry Me Again." I believe it is the question every wife is asking: "Would you marry me again?"

---

* www.dannyoertli.com

5:30 in the morning
Lying next to you
And you don't know that I'm watching you sleep
Just beside your pillow
On the nightstand by your hand
There's a picture there of you and me

We look so young how was I to know
Through the years how strong my love would grow

Will you marry me again
And give me your hand
And I'll give to you your old wedding band
Will you marry me again
And look in my eyes
And say the same words
That you did the first time
I love you more than I did back then
So will you marry me again

I knew the day I met you
I could see it in your smile
You were everything that I'd searched for
And I've found as we grow older
And the pages slowly turn
You are everything I wanted and more

So take this old bouquet that you have saved
Walk through the room just like you did that day

And marry me again
Give me your hand
I'll give to you your old wedding band
Will you marry me again
And look in my eyes
Say the same words
That you did the first time
I love you more than I did back then
I meant every word that I said back when
So marry me again
Marry me again

⭕ A WORD FROM THE WIVES

Here are wives' answers when they were asked to complete the sentence **"The best time we ever had as a couple was the time . . ."**

- "When we were pursuing one another and learning what was important to each of us."

- "When he plans surprise dates that are simple, like a picnic dinner, a drive by the ocean, or a moonlit walk."

- "Our honeymoon! He planned everything; even the destination was a surprise. He just told me what to pack. I loved watching all the little things he thought about for our honeymoon and all the thought he put into it. This made me feel so loved."

- "He planned a very romantic evening in a city we had traveled to for a wedding. It was amazing!"

CHAPTER HIGHLIGHTS

▶ Most of us were very intentional and imaginative in pursuing our wives and winning them over so they would marry us.

▶ Virtually every wife longs to be pursued and chosen after marriage.

▶ Many wives feel their husbands are no longer interested in them, because we fail to take initiative to spend time with them.

▶ If we are to continue to pursue them, we need to know them and what will make them feel special.

▶ Jesus pursued us and then continues to care for us after we are in His family.

▶ More marriages are destroyed by little things being ignored and eating away at the marriage than by catastrophic events.

▶ Anything we value and wish to maintain takes work—not dreaded work, but welcomed work, because of what we value.

GAME PLAN

o Give your wife a call or text her at least twice a day this week just to let her know you are thinking about her and wondering about how her day is going.

o Have flowers sent to her at home or office once this week, with a note: "Thanks for saying yes to me ___ years ago."

o Leave sticky notes on the bathroom mirror or some other place she will be able to read them when you leave the house or are gone on a trip, and let her know you are missing her.

o Plan a date for coffee, dinner, a movie, or some other type of event together. Let her know you desire to spend time with her.

o If you come up short on ideas, tell her you feel you have fallen down a bit in letting her know how much you love her, appreciate her, and want to spend time with her. Tell her you have some ideas for things to do, but would welcome any ideas she would like to share.

o Ask her what you could do today to let her know more fully how much you love her.

o Don't get discouraged if she doesn't respond as you wish right off. She may be in shock, or she may suspect you have something to confess to her or that you want something from her.

o Don't pursue her during the day and then pressure her to respond to you in bed. Your role is to love your wife in a Christ-like manner regardless of her response. Remember that the Church did not always respond well to Christ.

TALKIN' WITH THE BROTHERS

1. Tell each other one of the "best dates" you and your wife had when you were dating.

2. What were some of the things you did together in the early years of your relationship that seemed to bring you closer together?

3. Was there a time when you feel you stopped pursuing your wife?

4. Have you felt pursued by Christ in your life? If so, how so?

5. What is something you really value that you have worked hard to maintain?

6. What effect do you think your pursuit of your wife would have on your relationship?

7. What could you do this week that would help your wife feel more chosen or pursued by you?

DISCUSSING THE WORD

¹*"To the angel of the church in Ephesus write: 'The words of him who holds the seven stars in his right hand, who walks among the seven golden lampstands.*

²*" 'I know your works, your toil and your patient endurance, and how you cannot bear with those who are evil, but have tested those who call themselves apostles and are not, and found them to be false.* ³*I know you are enduring patiently and bearing up for my name's sake, and you have not grown weary.* ⁴*But I have this against you, that you have abandoned the love you had at first.* ⁵*Remember therefore from where you have fallen; repent, and do the works you did at first. If not, I will come to you and remove your lampstand from its place, unless you repent.' "*
—*Revelation 2:1–5*

1. What "good" things was the church in Ephesus doing? What would be the parallel for us in our marriages?

2. What did Jesus have against the church in Ephesus? What parallels might there be in our marriages?

3. What remedy did Jesus urge? What might be the parallel in our marriages?

6

Jesus Led the Church

But she doesn't seem to want to follow.

The couple had barely sat down in our counseling office when the husband said, "Tell my wife I am the head of the house and she needs to obey scripture. The Bible says she is to submit to me, and not to deprive me of sex, and that her body is mine."

After a pause, Virginia said, "Are there any other verses in scripture you know?"

Many men read in scripture, *"For the husband is the head of the wife"* (Ephesians 5:23) and then shut the Bible, saying, "That's enough scripture for today." They then take off on the word "head," from their experience; "head" means being in charge, telling others what to do, and having them wait on you. These men take their "corporate" definition of head and try to apply it to marriage. But scripture doesn't say "Husbands, love your wives, as secular management does"; it says *"Husbands, love your wives, as Christ loved the church"* (Ephesians 5:25). Christ stood the concept of leadership on its head. In a culture where women were little more than bought and sold commodities, Jesus elevated them to equal status with men *"since they are heirs with you."* (1 Peter 3:7)

Now, most of us are not as brazen as the husband described above, but if push came to shove we might have to admit we feel that being head of the home really is about our making the decisions. We should be able to do what we want to do, and everyone else should be willing to follow.

I recently received an email from a wife whose husband made the decision for their family to move to another state without consulting her. When I challenged the man, he said, "Sometimes a man's got to do what a man's got to do."

My response: "Well, this man—you—just did the wrong thing." The husband's responsibility is to discuss the issues of the decision together with his wife, and then make the decision based on what's best for his wife and family.

WHO *IS* THE HEAD OF THE HOME?

Many today debate whether husbands are to be in authority over their wives. They may say it depends on who makes the most money, who has the strongest personality, or who has the most intelligence. Others say there really is no one in authority in the marriage, but rather they should make all their decisions together—it is a 50-50 relationship.

When scripture says, *"Let us make man in our image"* (Genesis 1:26), there is no reason to believe the Father acted dictatorially; it was in conjunction with all members of the Trinity. However, in the Trinity there is an order when it comes to authority. Throughout scripture we see the Son being submissive to the Father, but that does not mean He is inferior to or less than the Father. It is impossible for any couple, ministry, or business to operate on a 50-50 basis. Someone must have ultimate responsibility and you cannot have ultimate responsibility unless you have ultimate authority.

When the apostle Paul writes in Ephesians 5:23 that the husband is the head of the wife, he goes on to clarify what he means by "head." Paul uses the big word *as* to clarify what "head of the wife" means. *"For the husband is the head of the wife even as Christ is the head of the church."* I have never heard a debate about whether the Church has authority over Christ or Christ over the Church. It is clear: Christ has been given authority over the Church, and thus, husbands have been given authority over their wives. Now, hold on before you break out the celebratory champagne. Christ's authority was *never* used for His own selfish ends. He *always* used his authority to lead and serve the Church.

THE POSITION OF LEADER

The difference between successful leaders and those who are not has a lot to do with their ability to bring alongside themselves people who are more gifted than they are in various areas. I know a number of business owners who are very successful because they have hired employees who know more than they do. That does not mean the smartest employee now becomes the president or owner of the company; it simply means the company has a wise owner. Insecure owners hire less talented employees so they will always be the smartest member of the company; or they unilaterally run the company, never seeking input from those who might threaten them. Most of those businesses fail to succeed. Virginia is way smarter and more talented than I am. She is certainly more outgoing and

> **CHRIST'S AUTHORITY WAS NEVER USED FOR HIS OWN SELFISH ENDS. HE *ALWAYS* USED HIS AUTHORITY TO LEAD AND SERVE THE CHURCH.**

better looking, but that does not mean she is the head of our home; it just means I am a "wise head" for asking her to marry me and be my partner.

When the two of us need to make a decision, there are many times that I will say something like, "We need to decide what school to enroll our girls in next fall. You have a much better grasp on this, and you actually liked school and did well in it. What do you think?"

People who are in effective partnerships do not spend time quibbling about who is the smartest or most gifted. They work together for the common good of the partnership.

WHEN DID THIS CO-OPERATION BECOME COMPETITION?

It all started in the Garden of Eden. God had created Adam, who had a perfect relationship with nature, with the animals, and with God. Sin had not yet entered the world. But in this perfect environment, God said, for the first time, that something was not good: it was not good that Adam was alone. So God gave Adam a "suitable helper" in Eve. When we think of the word "helper," we generally think of someone below us, someone to do our bidding, someone subservient. But that is not at all what this word means. The Hebrew word for "helper" used here is *ezer*. This word is used only 21 times in the Old Testament. Twice it is used to refer to Eve; three times it is used to refer to nations that provided military assistance to Israel; and the other 16 times it is used in reference to God as a helper. All of these verses are talking about a vital, powerful, and rescuing kind of help.

ADAM WAS HELD RESPONSIBLE FOR SIN ENTERING THE WORLD BECAUSE HE DID NOT PROTECT EVE OR RUN INTERFERENCE FOR HER.

So instead of God giving Eve to Adam to serve as a maid, what He was really saying was "Adam—you need help! It is not good for you to be alone. You need a partner who is like you and equal to you, but will come alongside you to make you better as a couple than you are as an individual."

God's desire was for Adam and Eve to work together as one. But Satan had other plans. In the Garden of Eden, Satan, in the form of a serpent, approached Eve individually to tempt her. Eve acted independently and did not ask Adam, to whom God had spoken directly, to clarify what His instructions were. Eve ate the fruit and gave some to Adam, "who was with her." But Adam was oblivious and not engaged; he just went along and ate the fruit as well, and the rest, as they say, is history. It may not seem fair, but from this point forward, it is Adam who is credited with the responsibility for sin entering the world, not Eve.

Therefore, just as sin came into the world through one man, and death through sin, and so death spread to all men because all sinned . . . —*Romans 5:12*

WITH LEADERSHIP COMES RESPONSIBILITY

Adam was held responsible for sin entering the world because he did not protect Eve or run interference for her. He followed her lead instead of leading her. This is why God speaks directly to Adam after the fall:

"Because you have listened to the voice of your wife and have eaten of the tree of which I commanded you, 'You shall not eat of it,' cursed is the ground because of you; in pain you shall eat of it all the days of your life . . ." —*Genesis 3:17*

The problem wasn't that Adam was listening to his wife share about her day; it was that Adam took his lead from Eve and listened to her *instead* of listening to God and leading her in what God had directly told him to do. Adam was silent! In the classic book *The Silence of Adam*, Larry Crabb describes what happened in the Garden and the ramifications we live with to this day:

> The silence of Adam is the beginning of every man's failure, from the rebellion of Cain to the impatience of Moses, from the weakness of Peter down to my failure yesterday to love my wife well. And it is a picture—a disturbing but revealing one—of the nature of our failure. Since Adam, every man has had a natural inclination to remain silent when he should speak. A man is most comfortable in situations in which he knows exactly what to do. When things get confusing and scary, his insides tighten and he backs away.
> —Larry Crabb, *The Silence of Adam*, pp. 11–12

The reason all of this is so critical is that instead of there being cooperation between Adam and Eve, there was now a power struggle, with Eve trying to usurp Adam's place as leader. This is shown in Genesis 3:16, where God spoke directly to Eve after her sin. He said to her, *"Your desire will be for your husband, and he will rule over you."* (Genesis 3:16, NIV). This desire is not a good desire; it is a desire to control. The only other place this word is used in the first five books of the Bible is in the next chapter when Cain and Abel are fighting and God says, *"Sin's desire is for you . . ."* Sin and Satan have no desire for relationship, but do have a desire to control.

FROM HELPER TO CONTROLLER

Wives, submit to your own husbands, as to the Lord . . . Husbands, love your wives, as Christ loved the church and gave himself up for her. —Ephesians 5:22, 25

As a result of sin entering the world, women's tendency is to try to control their husbands. Therefore, the apostle Paul says to them, "No, submit and respect them." Because of the fall, men's tendency is to misuse their authority either by acquiescing as Adam did or by using emotional or physical force to rule over their wives. Therefore, the apostle Paul says, "No, love your wives." You see, Ephesians 5 is the antidote, if you will, to the fall. It shows us how to get back to the original design for husband and wife.

I have written all of this because the subject of this chapter is leading your wife—and everything in our sin nature goes against us doing that well. Our wives' DNA also goes against that. Her tendency will be to try to control us, and ours is to be uninvolved, abdicating our position of head or attempting to rule over our wives in unhealthy ways.

ADAM? WHERE ARE YOU?

At the end of the day, God sought out Adam in the Garden after he and Eve had sinned. I don't think God called out for Adam because they were playing hide-and-seek. He called out for Adam because Adam was the head of the family.

And they heard the sound of the LORD God walking in the garden in the cool of the day, and the man and his wife hid themselves from the presence of the LORD *God among the trees of the garden. But the* LORD *God called to the man and said to him, "Where are you?" And he said, "I heard the sound of you in the garden, and I was afraid, because I was naked, and I hid myself." He said, "Who told you that you were naked? Have you eaten of the tree of which I commanded you not to eat?" The man said, "The woman whom you gave to be with me, she gave me fruit of the tree, and I ate."*

—*Genesis 3:8–12*

The text goes from using the plural "you" to using the singular "you," and also "man" and "he" rather than "the man and his wife" and "they." Adam was the appointed head of the unit, and God held him responsible. It is impossible to be responsible for something without having authority over it, and it is impossible to have authority over something without being responsible for it.

HUSBAND IS HEAD

Many wives say that they want their husbands to be responsible for the family but at the same time bristle when the husband exerts leadership in a way she does not agree with. Take a simple thing like going to the movies. You decide to show leadership and ask your wife out to see a movie—good start. You also want to be a serving husband, so you ask her what movie she wants to see. She says, "Oh, you pick. Anything is fine with me." So you pick the latest action movie. She says, "Not that!" So you settle on a more "refined" movie. You ask if she wants anything from the snack bar, and she says, "I'll just share whatever you get." So you get popcorn, and she says, "You didn't get it with butter, did you?" You then go into the theater and ask her where she wants to sit. She says, "Anywhere is fine with me." So you head to the top of the theater, and she says, "Not way up there!" . . . No wonder we give up!

Yet we are called to love our wives as Christ loved the Church, and part of that is leading our wives. Christ led the Church, yet the response of the Church was not always in agreement with His leadership. Listen to this exchange between Peter and Jesus as Jesus explains what He is about to do.

From that time Jesus began to show his disciples that he must go to Jerusalem and suffer many things from the elders and chief priests and scribes, and be killed, and on the third day be raised. And Peter took him aside and began to rebuke him, saying, "Far be it from you, Lord! This shall never happen to you." But he turned and said to Peter, "Get behind me, Satan! You are a hindrance to me. For you are not setting your mind on the things of God, but on the things of man."   —Matthew 16:21–23

Now, I am certainly not suggesting that when your wife challenges your leadership, you imitate Jesus exactly and tell her, "Get behind me, Satan! You are a hindrance to me." This will *definitely* not be helpful.

What I am suggesting is that we take initiative to lead and to seek God's direction, rather than just "going along" to make peace if we really feel a specific direction is best for our marriage or for the family.

I remember listening to a guest preacher from Korea trying to establish a connection with the U.S. congregation before he started to preach. He said, "I have only been in the States a short time, but I have learned the two most important words a husband is to say: 'Yes, dear.'" The congregation laughed, but I believe God was not laughing. As I travel and speak, I find many men in their 60s, 70s, and 80s who have become what I call "Yes, dear" men. They are sweet and nice, don't yell or argue, and live with their wives peacefully, but there is no intimacy, no vitality, no life. They walked away from their masculinity years ago, and they hate their life—and their wives resent that they do not lead.

Robert Bly, a well-known and respected author, put it this way:

In the seventies I began to see all over the country a phenomenon that we might call the "soft male." Sometimes even today when I look out at an audience, perhaps half the young males are what I'd call soft. They're lovely, valuable people—I like them—they're not interested in harming the earth or starting wars. There's a gentle attitude toward life in their whole being and style of living. But many of these men are not happy. You quickly notice the lack of energy in them. They are life-preserving but not exactly life-giving. Ironically, you often see these men with strong women who positively radiate energy.   —Robert Bly, *Iron John*

TAKE INITIATIVE

Many of us have become paralyzed by being afraid we won't lead well, so we don't lead at all. What I believe many women want is simply for us to take some initiative and engage.

Far too many of us succumb to just asking our wives to tell us what they want. This may seem generous at first, but again, it is not really what they want. For instance, say you come home and it is clear it has not been a good day for your wife, so you say, "What do you want to do for dinner tonight? Do you want to go out? Where do you want to go?" You may wonder what's wrong with that. Well, you have just put the burden of all the decision-making on your wife. I would suggest that when you come home and see such a situation, you say, "Looks like it's been a hard day. Let's go out for dinner tonight. How about that new Mexican place down the street?" You have taken initiative. She may say, "Oh, I ate there with some friends yesterday; how about Chinese?" You say, "Great." Seems very similar, but just taking a little leadership and initiative and then listening to her wishes and accommodating them will go a long way toward making your wife feel cared for and led.

A WORD FROM THE WIVES

Here are wives' answers when asked to complete the sentence, **"When it comes to leadership in our relationship, I wish my husband . . ."**

- "Pursued me, took initiative."
- "Would take more of a role in it."
- "Took some. He always has said 'whatever you want' and when I would ask him for advice he would say, 'whatever you think is best.' It feels very lonely."
- "Would take the lead in having the difficult talks with our boys."
- "Would not leave so many decisions to me. He says whatever I want to do or wherever I go is okay with him, but sometimes I think he doesn't really like what I decide. In other words, I don't think he is completely honest with me."
- "Would actively do things to show he loves me and cares for me without me needing to ask all the time for him to do things. I wish he would initiate even more dates or times alone. Basically I feel it comes down to I wish he would act like he did when we were dating—trying to woo my heart, making me feel loved and special, and showing a deep desire to be with me. Now, after 15 years, so much of that is lost and I feel that there is no more leadership in the relationship."
- "Would lead! I coordinate our lives and he seems to just be along for the ride."
- "Was the leader of our family. I know God would bless us through him if he would take the lead."

CHAPTER HIGHLIGHTS

▶ Even in the perfect, sinless Garden of Eden, God said it was not good for Adam to be alone, that he needed a partner.

▶ God gave Adam the directions on how to live in the Garden.

▶ Because Adam and Eve did not consult each other, they fell prey to the schemes of Satan.

▶ Even though Eve was first to eat the fruit, Adam is held responsible for sin entering the world because he did not protect Eve.

▶ Because of sin entering the world, Eve and all her female descendants tend to try to control their husbands.

▶ Because of sin entering the world, Adam and all his male descendants have a tendency either to abdicate their leadership role or to use their authority to rule over their wives.

▶ What God designed for unity and cooperation is now a relationship of strife and the desire for power.

▶ Ephesians 5 is the antidote to the fall; it instructs men not to rule over their wives but to love them, and instructs wives not to control their husbands but to submit to them and respect them.

▶ The husband is given the position of head in the family just as Jesus is given the position of head over the Church.

▶ Jesus never used His authority for His own ends, and neither should we as husbands.

▶ Our wives long for us to lead, but sometimes even when we do, they challenge our leadership.

► It is easy to simply withdraw and let our wife lead, but this is neglecting our call to be the head of the wife.

► Being positional, "head" does not mean we are smarter or always have better ideas.

► Often, simply taking initiative is what is needed when leading.

GAME PLAN

○ Tell your wife you want to be more the leader God calls you to be and that you want to apologize for not always being a protector and servant-leader in the family.

○ Take the initiative in starting a discussion on finances, vacation, education, or something you have avoided in the past.

○ Call your wife from work and say you would like to take the family out to dinner tonight or tomorrow and name a restaurant. If she has another suggestion, go with it and thank her for the idea.

○ Arrange for childcare, if you have children, and tell your wife you would like for the two of you to get away for an evening out together. Suggest an activity you know she would enjoy: perhaps it would be a long walk, stargazing, bowling, dancing, or a concert. Be creative!

If you haven't done anything like the above in the past, your wife might resist or question your motives. Don't get discouraged and give up. It may take some time and consistency on your part to regain her trust and grow in intimacy.

TALKIN' WITH THE BROTHERS

1. How was leadership in the home expressed when you grew up?

2. What do you think most men think of when they are described as head of the home?

3. What are some subtle or not so subtle ways wives try to "control" their husbands?

4. What strikes you about the Biblical explanation of the husband being the "head of the wife"?

5. What is the greatest challenge to you being the leader at home?

6. Share ways you have led at home that have seemed to work well.

7. What one thing could you do this week to be a more Christ-like leader at home?

DISCUSSING THE WORD

⁶So when the woman saw that the tree was good for food, and that it was a delight to the eyes, and that the tree was to be desired to make one wise, she took of its fruit and ate, and she also gave some to her husband who was with her, and he ate. ⁷Then the eyes of both were opened, and they knew that they were naked. And they sewed fig leaves together and made themselves loincloths.

⁸And they heard the sound of the Lord *God walking in the garden in the cool of the day, and the man and his wife hid themselves from the presence of the* Lord *God among the trees of the garden. ⁹But the* Lord *God called to the man and said to him, "Where are you?" ¹⁰And he said, "I heard the sound of you in the garden, and I was afraid, because I was naked, and I hid myself." ¹¹He said, "Who told you that you were naked? Have you eaten of the tree of which I commanded you not to eat?" ¹²The man said, "The woman whom you gave to be with me, she gave me fruit of the tree, and I ate."*   —Genesis 3:6–12

1. In what way did Adam fail to lead in the Garden of Eden? How might this be similar to how we are tempted not to lead in our marriages?

2. What were the results of Adam's failure to lead? How might this be true in our marriages?

3. Why do you think God called out to Adam first and not Eve?

4. How do we often imitate Adam when confronted with our failure?

7

Jesus Loved and Served the Church Sacrificially

Yeah, but that got Him nailed to a cross

The story is told of the pig and the chicken that wanted to fix a special breakfast for their owner's family. As they discussed the menu, the chicken said, "Let's each contribute something to the meal. How about if I contribute the eggs and you contribute the bacon?"

"That's easy for you to say," said the pig. "For you it's a contribution; for me it's total sacrifice."

If we were honest, when it comes to loving our wives, we would often prefer to make a "contribution" rather than a "total sacrifice."

Certainly there is no greater example of "love" than Christ's sacrifice: His death on the cross for our sake.

"Greater love has no one than this, that someone lay down his life for his friends." —John 15:13

Love, in its most pure sense, is sacrificial, with the other person's best in mind. I recall a man coming up to me after I presented this concept of sacrificial love in marriage and he said, "Die for my wife? That's easy. It's *living* with her that's killing me!" And that is true for most of us. We actually *would* give our lives for the sake of our wife— but not go golfing? Come on, man!

WHAT IS LOVE?

Sacrificial love that puts the needs and desires of another before yourself is quite foreign to our "have it your way" culture. I recently talked to a man who was having an affair with a younger woman. When I confronted him about the damage his actions would have on his marriage and the pain it would cause his wife and children, he said, "Well, I don't want to live the rest of my life in a 'sterilized' marriage." When I asked what he meant by that, he said, "I don't think I should have to give up working on my cars on the weekend and flying my plane when I want, just because I'm supposed to spend time with my wife and children." I later found out that he left for work every day before the kids were awake, and stayed out to drink with friends until 9 or so each evening.

Another husband shared that his therapist said he needed to take care of himself and pursue whatever or whoever really made him happy. Shortly after he finished speaking, Virginia and I suggested that pursuing his own happiness might seem attractive at first, but we believed that at the deepest level we were designed to sacrificially love and that this is truly what will give us the most satisfaction and joy—much more so than pursuing our own selfish happiness. Overcome with the sudden realization of this truth, the man bowed his head and started sobbing. Being selfish will never satisfy what our soul longs for.

Gary Thomas puts it so well in his profound book, *Sacred Marriage*:

> Any situation that calls me to confront my selfishness has enormous spiritual value, and I slowly began to understand that the real purpose of marriage may not be happiness as much as it is holiness . . . If the purpose of marriage was simply to enjoy an infatuation and make me "happy," then I'd have to get a "new" marriage every two or three years.
>
> —Gary Thomas, *Sacred Marriage*, pp. 22, 23

Now, you may say, "At least I am not having an affair," but let's look a bit closer at what sacrificial love might look like on a practical, daily basis.

LOVE, EVERYDAY STYLE

Let's say, for instance, that I love playing golf, but Virginia hates golf. I tell her that this coming Saturday I am going to take her golfing. Do I get love points for that? Obviously not. Imagine that I love golf and she likes it okay. Do I get love points for that? Perhaps a few, but I am still doing what I want to do. Suppose I tell her I have cancelled my tee time and am going to spend the day shopping with her. That's love!

My mentor, John Tebay, tells of waking up on a Saturday morning and over breakfast asking his wife Grace what she wanted to do that day. Her response was that she would really like John to go shopping with her for a white blouse. John said, "Okay, let's go."

So off they went to T.J. Maxx. They walked to the "white blouse" section. Grace picked one up and asked John if he liked it.

"Love it," he said.

"I like it also," was her response.

John turned and walked ahead of Grace to the cash registers, only to turn around and see Grace *without* the white blouse.

"I thought you liked that one," he said.

"Oh, I did," she remarked, "but I am not sure it is *the one*."

So off they went to Marshalls, Macy's, and J. C. Penney, only to return home without a blouse. When they pulled into their driveway Grace thanked John for coming and said how much she enjoyed their morning shopping together. Later, John said to me, "She didn't really want to buy a blouse—she just wanted to *look* at them. We are sure different! If I want to buy a crescent wrench, I go to the hardware store, find one, buy it, and return home. Mission accomplished."

As much as we would like to say, "What's wrong with that woman?" we need to simply smile and say, "We sure are different." So in order to love our wife sacrificially, we really do need to know what it is that makes them come alive, and then go and do that with or for them.

HEART TRANSPLANT

There is no better example that I know of regarding learning how to love than Lou and Grace. Lou and Grace had been married thirty years when Lou told Grace that he had never loved her. Soon after this, Lou and Grace separated. From a human standpoint, they should never have been married. Lou was raised in foster homes and orphanages. He was a big-machinery diesel mechanic and loved anything that made loud noises and involved grease and dirt. He loved to go to drag races and rodeos on his days off. Grace, on the other hand, was Dutch in every sense of the word. Her hair was never out of place, and she dressed impeccably. She never had a speck of dirt on her, and she loved going to quilting exhibits and craft shows.

SACRIFICIAL LOVE WILL INVOLVE, IN SOME WAY, KNOWING YOUR WIFE'S DESIRES AND CHEERFULLY DOING SOMETHING TO MEET THOSE DESIRES.

After a year and a half of separation, they got back together, hoping to save their marriage.

That Christmas we went to The Nutcracker ballet with Lou and Grace. During the intermission, I went up to Lou and said, "So, you like ballet, do you?" He looked me straight in the eyes and said, "I love my wife." And that is the right answer. You see, Lou felt about ballet the same way our youngest daughter, Julie, did. When we asked her how she liked the ballet, she said, "It was fine, except for the dancing." But Lou now goes to ballets, craft shows, and quilting exhibits, and Grace goes to rodeos and drag races—not because their preferences have changed, but because their hearts have changed. And those two hearts just celebrated their 60th wedding anniversary! After the celebration, with close to 200 of their friends and family—including 3 children, 7 grandchildren, and 12 great-grandchildren, Grace told Virginia, "I sure am glad we stayed together!" So are we, and so are countless others!

Contrast this with the wife who loved ballet and asked her husband to go with her to a performance. "Listen, I'll do better than that," he replied. "I'll buy you season tickets to the theater and you can take any girlfriend you wish. I'll even get a driver for you and pay for dinner." With tears streaming down her face she said, "You don't get it. I just want to go with you occasionally."

So what will it look like for you? Seeing a chick flick, going to a museum, taking a long walk, or just cuddling? Sacrificial love will involve, in some way, knowing your wife's desires and cheerfully doing something to meet those desires. I say "cheerfully," because too many husbands, if they do go and do something with their wife, complain the whole time, play with their phone, or tell her how much she owes him for what he is doing. If you are going to do it, do it with a cheerful attitude—it will go a lot further in helping your wife feel loved.

SACRIFICIAL LOVE THROUGH SERVING

Virginia and I were leading a family mission trip in Trinidad with eight other families when Pastor Ashoke, our host, came to brief us on our daily activities. "Today we have a special treat for you to observe: a Trinidadian wedding! And Paul will be officiating." That was news to me! I protested, saying I had never even met the couple, but Ashoke prevailed, assuring me he would do all of the ceremony except the message, but he wanted me to do that part of the service. In the Trinidadian tradition, the couple sit on chairs facing the pastor during the ceremony. I think this is for two reasons. One is they actually expect the couple to listen to what the pastor says, unlike U.S. weddings where the bride and groom are usually just staring at each other, giggling, fixing their hair, and whispering, "I love you." The second reason is that they expect the message will be more like a full-blown sermon than a devotional thought.

The time in the service came when I was to address the couple, a 19-year-old male and a 16-year-old female. I started talking about God's design for marriage generally, and then individually addressed the bride and groom. I quoted from Ephesians 5 about the wife submitting and respecting her husband, and the groom was all smiles. Then I addressed him directly and said he was to love his wife as Christ loved the Church, and part of that meant he was to be the chief servant in the home—at which point the young man literally crossed his arms over his chest, in essence silently screaming, "*Nooooo! I thought she was to serve me!*"

If we are honest, most of us entered marriage with a perspective similar to that of this Trinidadian groom. "The wife is to serve me and make my life easier, more fun, and less lonely." I know that was true for me. If I am really honest, I would say some of my unspoken expectations for marriage were that Virginia would be someone to cook for me, have sex with me, encourage me, have sex with me, watch movies with me, have sex with me, clean the house, and have sex with me. What's so unrealistic about that?

The unrealistic part is that it is not Biblical. Not that marriage cannot improve our state of life; it certainly did mine. And Virginia has served me, cared for me, encouraged me, and had sex with me. But at the end of the day, I am called to use my authority to serve my wife and put her interests above my own.

BUT DO YOU KNOW WHO I AM?

For a number of years now, Virginia and I have run a weekly Bible study during the NFL season for our team's players here in New England. We are often amused to hear stories about their interactions at home. A player may have just come home from a last-minute victory in which he caught the winning pass, tossed the winning touchdown, made the interception that won the game, made the block that allowed the winning run, or blocked the field goal that would have cost the game. He walks into the house, and his wife says, "Would you take out the trash? It's overflowing again." And he is tempted to think, or stupid enough to say, "Do you know who I am?" to which she says, "Yeah, you're my husband. Now take out the trash."

If ever there was a man to say "Do you know who I am?" that would win Him the "get out of serving" card, it would be Jesus. One of my favorite stories in scripture is the one about Jesus washing the disciples' feet. The expectation in those times was that when you went to eat somewhere, upon entering the house, a servant would wash your feet before you lay on your side to eat. Well, Jesus and

His disciples had arrived at an upper room to have a special meal together, and there was no servant to greet them and wash their feet.

It is important to note that not long before this, the disciples had been arguing among themselves over who was the greatest in the group. Actually, everyone knew that Jesus was the greatest, so they were really arguing about who was the *second* greatest in the room. We pick up the story in John 13:

> *Jesus, knowing that the Father had given all things into his hands, and that he had come from God and was going back to God, rose from supper. He laid aside his outer garments, and taking a towel, tied it around his waist. Then he poured water into a basin and began to wash the disciples' feet and to wipe them with the towel that was wrapped around him . . .*
>
> *When he had washed their feet and put on his outer garments and resumed his place, he said to them, "Do you understand what I have done to you? You call me Teacher and Lord, and you are right, for so I am. If I then, your Lord and Teacher, have washed your feet, you also ought to wash one another's feet. For I have given you an example, that you also should do just as I have done to you. Truly, truly, I say to you, a servant is not greater than his master, nor is a messenger greater than the one who sent him. If you know these things, blessed are you if you do them."* —*John 13:3–5, 12–17*

Can you imagine being there and being one of the disciples? Remember, they had just been arguing about which of them was the greatest. This is what I imagine went through their minds as they entered the room and realized someone needed to wash feet. "Okay, I may not be the greatest, but I sure as heck am not going to admit I am the least by doing a servant's job." There was an awkward milling around, maybe even some looking at one or more of the less "prominent" disciples and pointing to the basin. And then, Jesus *"laid aside his outer garments, and taking a towel, tied it around his waist. Then he poured water into a basin and began to wash the disciples' feet . . ."* (John 13:4–5).

I bet every disciple at that point was thinking, "Man, I wish I had thought of doing that!"

You see, "... *the Son of Man* [Christ] *came not to be served but to serve...*" (Mark 10:45). After serving them, Jesus reminded them that He had done this as an example for them and they were to do as He had done. Then He added that last sentence: *"If you know these things, blessed are you if you do them."* We are not blessed just by *knowing* the truth; we are blessed when we *act* on the truth.

SERVING IS ALLURING

After speaking at a marriage conference in which we included a section on husbands serving their wives, a woman came up afterward and said she wanted to share a story that affirmed what we were teaching. She told us that when her husband serves her, it makes him more sexually attractive to her. "In fact," she said, "when I see him scrubbing the toilet I just want to rip his shirt off and make passionate love with him." I bet that house had the cleanest toilets in town!

As we have said many times already, we serve because that is what we are called to do, not manipulatively for the response. However, my experience has been that a serving husband is very attractive to most wives. So, get out the toilet brush!

SACRIFICIAL LOVE IN THE BEDROOM

"Okay, now this is taking it *too far*. I am willing to serve my wife in the kitchen by doing dishes, I will vacuum the living room, I will even clean the bathroom, but the bedroom is the one room where she is supposed to serve me!! Doesn't the Bible tell her not to deprive me? Isn't this one area I can demand what I need? I mean, if we don't have sex, I won't be able to concentrate at work and might lose my job and then we will lose our house and be homeless out on the street!"

And they say women are overly dramatic?

I have heard men tell their wives that if they don't have sex they will die. Sorry, but no man has ever died from his testicles exploding! If I were speaking at a women's conference or if Virginia and I were speaking at a marriage conference, we would certainly tell the women about how very important sex is to a man—but since this book is for men, let me focus here for a bit. Loving our wives sacrificially in the sexual area means thinking of her before we think of ourselves.

This is tough, because men and women think about sex so differently. I tend to reason, "If I like it, she should like it." But often she doesn't. In fact, if we were to do just what comes naturally to us, we could be "satisfied" and our wife would still be wondering when we were going to start making love.

There is one book in the Bible devoted almost exclusively to the subject of marital sexuality: the Song of Solomon. In chapter 2, verse 6, and again in chapter 8, verse 3, the exact same phrase is used: *"His left hand is under my head, and his right hand embraces me."* The word translated "embrace" literally means to stimulate or fondle. In the very next

FOR MOST WOMEN, RELATIONAL CLOSENESS IS "FOREPLAY."

verse, the new wife tells her single friends, *"I adjure you, O daughters of Jerusalem, that you not stir up or awaken love until it pleases."* What Solomon is saying is "I take care of my wife before taking care of myself." The response of his wife is to tell her friends, "This is so powerful, do not do this unless you are married."

The point for us as husbands is to focus on how we are able to please our wives before thinking about ourselves. Since for most women, relational closeness is "foreplay," we need to ask ourselves, "How can I show my wife I love her in ways she will understand?" Physically, it means, "How can I bring pleasure to her before just thinking of myself?" Here is the irony. The wife in the Song of Solomon is saying, "Ladies, when my man takes care of me, it makes him irresistible." Again, this is not to be used to manipulate. No, we love our wives because we are called to do that, even when they do not immediately respond.

Loving our wives sacrificially in this area may mean simply taking her at her word that she does have a headache or is really too tired. Perhaps it means we do more to assist around the house so she truly isn't so spent at night.

GOD'S DESIGN FOR SACRIFICIAL LOVE IS BEST FOR ALL INVOLVED

We were in Portland, Oregon, speaking at a couples' conference. Our last talk of the day was on marital sexuality. After the evening session ended, one husband turned to his wife and said, "Want to go to bed?" She responded, "I think we should talk about how our marriage is doing." They got into an argument and he stormed off to their room while she hung around—and soon after, shared with us their encounter. Later that night, I was walking through the lobby of this beautiful four-star resort and noticed her sitting there, quietly reading a book by herself. I thought to myself how sad it was that neither of them got what they wanted that night. When he said "Let's go to bed," he was saying he wanted to make love. When she said "Let's talk," she wanted to connect relationally with him—and neither desire was realized.

SACRIFICIALLY SERVE YOUR WIFE, AND PREPARE TO BE BLESSED!

How different it could have been! When she said to her husband, "Let's talk," he could have responded, "Sure, if that's what you want. Let's go get some coffee." I can almost guarantee that after meaningful connection through conversation, she would have felt connected to him and much more inclined to make love. Or, when he said to his wife, "Let's go to bed," she could have responded with "Sure, let's go make love—we can always talk tomorrow." (I don't think it would ever happen, but I do want to at least present it as a possibility for illustration purposes.)

You see, when we put the interests of our spouse ahead of our own, we actually benefit as well. I am not speaking about manipulation, as in: "I talked to you for two hours, you owe me 15 minutes." No, we listen and talk because we love our wife and it is the right thing to do. It's likely that our wives, when loved well, will respond in kind.

SACRIFICIAL LOVE IS A DECISION OF THE WILL

We have a daily choice to do that which gives life or that which damages our marriage. One of the wives we surveyed expressed it well when she emailed me the following birthday story:

> My husband feels that romance is too sentimental and often devoid of real meaning. However, he knows that I don't share his sentiments and would prefer that romance was more a part of our relationship. . . . When I had a milestone birthday a few years back, he managed to press through his ambivalence and love me well. Without any prodding from me, he organized a fabulous celebration complete with beautiful decorations, food, original party games, and more. I have never felt more loved by him and will truly cherish this memory for the remainder of my life.

For I have given you an example, that you also should do just as I have done to you . . . If you know these things, blessed are you if you do them.
　　　　　　　　　　　　　　　　　　　—John 13:15, 17

Sacrificially serve your wife, and prepare to be blessed! I would say, in fact, that without sacrificial love it will be impossible to experience the joy in marriage we all long for.

A WORD FROM THE WIVES

In our survey it was surprising that one of the items that kept surfacing was the way husbands serving their wives sacrificially had such an impact. Again, the types of service were not huge, but made a huge impression.

Here are wives' answers when asked to complete the sentence **"I feel most loved by my husband when . . .":**

- "He notices I have done something and takes the time to compliment me on it."
- "He reassures me that he loves being married to me."
- "I feel loved by him when he helps around the house."
- "I feel most loved by my husband when he helps me. And it doesn't even have to be something big! It could be anything— setting the dining room table, picking up the kids from an activity, carrying laundry upstairs, getting me a glass of water, or emptying the recycling. That's when I know he's thinking of me and what he could do to help me."
- "I feel loved by him when he helps me in the kitchen."
- "I feel cared for by him when he serves me by doing something around the house or for me that I know he doesn't care about at all and is only doing because he loves me."
- "When I arrived home late after an unexpected meeting, and dinner was all made. After dinner I sat down on the couch just to rest for a few minutes and fell fast asleep for a while. Usually our routine is that whoever cooks, the other cleans up. Well, when I woke up, he was up doing the dishes. I offered to help, but he said, 'No, honey, you rest, I'm happy to clean up.'"

CHAPTER HIGHLIGHTS

► Love is most fully expressed through sacrifice.

► Christ's sacrificial death on the cross is the greatest expression of love known to man.

► Love is expressed practically by knowing the desires of your mate and making them happen.

► Love often has more to do with a change of heart than simply a change of action.

► Since we have been given authority in the home, we can use it to benefit others.

► No matter who we are, One greater than us has given the example of how to serve.

► We have the authority to put others before ourselves in practical, everyday situations.

► A man who serves is much more attractive to a woman than one who does not.

► We were created to serve—and actually find the most joy when we do.

► Husbands are called to love their wives sacrificially in the bedroom as well as the living room.

► Ultimately, love has more to do with our will than our hormones.

► When we love sacrificially, we actually benefit as well.

GAME PLAN

Don't try to do these all at once; just pick two or three to start.

o   When she goes out for the evening or to an event, do the dishes without her asking.

o   Ask her before you leave in the morning if there is anything you could do for her today.

o   Get up early and fix breakfast for the family on a Saturday and waken them to a fully cooked meal—or get take-out if your own cooking would not be seen as serving them well.

o   Put the toilet seat down.

o   Pick up the children on your way home so she doesn't have to go out.

o   Tell her you are taking the kids out for dinner and putting them to bed on a specific day next week so she can have the evening free to do what she wishes.

o   Give her a coupon good for one day of "anything you would like me to do for or with you."

o   Fill the car she drives with gas.

o   Wash and clean the car she drives.

o   Clean the toilet.

TALKIN' WITH THE BROTHERS

1. What thoughts come to mind when you hear the word "sacrifice"?

2. In what ways was the death of Christ such a pure expression of sacrificial love?

3. In what practical ways does your having authority in the home allow you to serve more fully?

4. Why does loving your wife sacrificially in the bedroom often seem like such a challenge?

5. Tell of a time where you felt you really loved your wife sacrificially.

6. What effect did your taking the initiative of sacrificial love have on your relationship?

7. Each man share one way you could more fully serve and express sacrificial love to your wife this week.

DISCUSSING THE WORD

25But Jesus called them to him and said, "You know that the rulers of the Gentiles lord it over them, and their great ones exercise authority over them. 26It shall not be so among you. But whoever would be great among you must be your servant, 27and whoever would be first among you must be your slave, 28even as the Son of Man came not to be served but to serve, and to give his life as a ransom for many."

—Matthew 20:25–28

1. All husbands have been given positions of authority in the home. How should a Christ-following husband differ from someone who doesn't know Christ in the use of this authority?

2. In practical terms, what does imitating Christ as the servant look like in your marriage?

3. "*Husbands, love your wives, as Christ loved the church . . .*" What does "giving your life" for your wife look like in your daily life?

8

Jesus Led the Church Spiritually

Now, that's a real guilt-producer!

For many couples, their spiritual life—or lack thereof—is an area of tension. One of the most common complaints we hear from wives who are Christ-followers is "My husband isn't the spiritual leader in our home."

When Virginia and I were first married, I was committed to being the spiritual leader in our marriage. So I read the Bible and then basically told Virginia how the passage applied to her. This was not received well. We soon settled into a rhythm of each of us doing our own personal study and then sharing with each other, along with praying together daily.

I do know a few couples that actually have regular Bible studies together, but it is rare. There are a few more that read a devotional together each day, such as *Daily Bread*, *Jesus Calling*, or our current favorite, *New Morning Mercies*, and then pray. As we travel and speak and poll couples, asking if they have a regular time of shared Bible study or prayer times, we find the response extremely low. Family Life® has surveyed thousands of Christian couples and found that less than 8% of them pray together on a regular basis. *

---

* https://www.familylife.com/articles/topics/marriage/staying-married/
growing-spiritually/one-simple-habit-that-will-transform-your-marriage/

In our estimation, that is even a higher percentage than what we have found.

Although statistics vary, the divorce rate in the United States is widely quoted as being between 35% and 50%. But a Gallup poll revealed that among married couples who pray together daily, the divorce rate is 1 out of 1,153 (less than 1%). If regular prayer together is so critical to the vitality of the marriage, it should be no surprise why the evil one is going to do everything he can to discourage us from praying together. Yet if we men are to imitate Christ, we are called to "wash our wives in the word" and take the lead for the spiritual atmosphere in our home.

Husbands, love your wives, as Christ loved the church and gave himself up for her, that he might sanctify her, having cleansed her by the washing of water with the word . . .   —Ephesians 5:25

I often wonder why God gave husbands the role of spiritual leader. In my experience, women tend to gravitate toward spiritual things more than men. If a church has a small-group Bible study for women, our wives will want to go. Women seem to love to get together and talk. But men, not so much. We tend to shy away from small groups that mostly involve talking.

You see this even at social gatherings. If a woman needs to use the restroom, she often gets up and announces "I'm going to the ladies room. Does anyone want to join me?" And immediately three other women jump up. It's a group experience. I have never seen a man get up and say, "I'm going to the bathroom—any guys want to join me?"

But whether it comes naturally or not, we as husbands are called to lead. When we hear "lead spiritually" we tend to break out in a cold sweat. I think that is often because we have a mental image of spirituality that feels quite feminine. We think that real spiritual people are more expressive emotionally: they hold their hands up in worship, they love reading God's word whenever they have a free moment, their prayers tend to be colorful and lengthy, and so on. The critical issue is not matching our wives' spiritual routines, but finding a rhythm that works for us and helps us follow the Lord more fully.

WHY COUPLES DON'T PRAY TOGETHER

If prayer is talking with God, which it is, then it should be consistent with our patterns of communication as individuals. I am a man of few words, and let's just say Virginia is more "thorough" in her communication. When she asks me how my day was, I say "Fine." "Fine" is a complete sentence to me. When I ask her how *her* day was, I get a much fuller answer.

I tend to be more task-oriented, while Virginia tends to be more relationally-oriented. So it makes sense that when I pray, I tend to pray succinctly, focused on the "task," while she prays more thoroughly, focused on the bigger picture. I might pray something like, "Lord, a few things on my mind today: please watch over our family and help me with the speech I am giving." Virginia, on the other hand, will tend to pray something like this. "Oh, most gracious heavenly Father, when I look out and see the cumulus clouds and the incredible blue sky, I am reminded of your love for us . . .". It is beautiful, but she may take five minutes getting to the "issues" to pray about.

> **WHEN WE FAIL OR HAVE DIFFICULTY IN OUR WORKPLACE, WE TRY HARDER TO IMPROVE, BUT WHEN WE FEEL RIDICULED OR FAIL AT HOME, WE QUIT.**

Many couples struggle simply because of differences in the length of their prayers. Most men can cover pretty much everything they are thinking about in 45 seconds or so. Their wife starts to pray and after 15 minutes she is just getting to South Africa as she is praying around the globe and her husband is snoring. She looks over at him and says, "Spiritual pygmy!" and they never pray together again. I don't know what it is about us men, but when we fail or have difficulty in our workplace, we try harder to improve, but when we feel ridiculed or fail at home, we quit.

In his great book, *Blessed Are the Misfits*, author and radio personality Brant Hansen writes,

> When God became a man, when He took on flesh and walked among us, He stood in front of a crowd and told them how to pray in Matthew 6. The crowd lived in a religion-soaked culture, wherein lengthy public prayers were the order of the day and were associated with rightness with God. Jesus says, "Here's how to pray..." and He then prays for about 25 seconds. And then quits!
> —Brant Hansen, *Blessed Are the Misfits*, p. 71

Jesus is clearly more interested in the posture of our heart than in the length of our prayers.

• Temperament differences

Some couples' temperaments get in the way. One may be very structured and have a daily reading schedule, while the other is much more free-flowing; one loves to process thoughts out loud, while the other is very private; one has a specific time and place for devotions, while the other tries to fit it in some time and some place; one loves to journal, while the other has no interest in writing anything because God knows his thoughts.

• Differences in daily routines

Many couples struggle with daily rhythms in various areas, but this can really affect the couple if their clocks seem to be set differently. One may get up in the morning and exclaim enthusiastically, "Good morning, Lord!" The other, reaching for the coffee maker, mumbles, "Good Lord, it's morning!" One person may reason that since Jesus got up early to pray, we should, too. The other finds that praying at the end of the day works best. Virginia enjoys a reading plan and devotional book for her devotions. I do better when I am working on something—a topic or theme—and researching it.

• Fear of being preached at

Many men I know avoid devotional books with their wives because they are pretty sure they are going to get thrown under the bus at some point. We tend not to initiate conversations when we have an idea where the end of the conversation will go. I tend not to bring up my eating habits or exercise routines with Virginia because I know I will be on the short end of that stick.

By now you may be thinking that you are like the man who went to the doctor for heartburn and the doctor gave him a list of things that cause heartburn. He said, "Doc, I know what *causes* heartburn, I have it. I want to know what to take to *cure* it!"

TIPS FOR PRAYING TOGETHER †

• Pick a specific time and make a commitment.

I am not a structured person, but I do know that if prayer time is "whenever" it is often just "never." Get in bed together and pray, even if one of you is a night owl and will get up after you have finished praying. Wake up and pray together, even if one goes back to sleep when the other gets up. For many couples, simply asking "How can I pray for you today?" as you leave the house, and then taking a minute to pray for each other, works well. The time is not critical, the prayer is.

• Don't be upset if you miss a day.

If you have a busy day and miss a meal, you don't say, "Fine, that's it! I can't even plan enough time to eat. I am never eating again." If you miss a meal, you eat the next one. So if you miss a day of prayer together, hit the next one.

• Decide who will do what.

It sounds so simple, but who initiates is often an obstacle. Just as the disciples sat around waiting for someone to wash their feet, many couples sit around waiting for who will suggest praying together. One suggestion we found helpful was to alternate: one spouse initiates prayer on the even days and one on the odd. We suggest men on the odd, since we are usually a bit more odd. The one rule is, if it is not your day, you can't remind your mate. So it's off-limits for your wife to say:

---

† Some of these tips have been adapted from David and Jan Stoop's book *When Couples Pray Together*, published by Regal Books.

"Honey, do you know what day it is?"

"Tuesday?"

"No, what *number* day it is?"

"The 19th?"

"Would you say that is an even number or an odd number?"

"Odd."

"Do you remember what you are to initiate on the odd days of the month, or would you like me to tell you, you moron?"

Instead, if you forget to initiate prayer on your day, ask your wife to not say anything. Her day is tomorrow, and likely if she keeps all her days, you will be praying 50% more than you used to. I also suspect you will start remembering what day it is and start leading in prayer.

- **Set realistic expectations.**

I am an all-or-nothing sort of guy, so on January 1, I'm all in: exercise an hour every day, read and pray an hour, then go to work. Before too many days elapse, I'm a nothing sort of guy, because my expectations were not realistic. Set realistic goals for your spiritual life with your wife. "Hey, babe, could we set as a goal saying a quick prayer for each other before we head out the door in the morning and praying together for our family when we head to bed?" I doubt she will criticize you for too small an effort; rather, she will be delighted that you have initiated some time together with the Lord.

- **Agree that neither one of you will preach in your praying.**

"And Lord, please help Bill to be more careful in what he eats and become more disciplined in his exercise so he takes care of his body, Your temple."

"And Lord, you know that Sally was rude to my mom last week. Please help her to see that Mom did not mean any harm when she asked if everyone in Sally's family was overweight."

We need to remember that we are talking to God, not our spouse. My suggestion is that if you are praying for change, pray for change in *you*. Unite together in prayer for mutual concerns instead of uniting with the evil one in bringing division and strife.

THE IMPORTANCE OF MODELING

It has been said that more is caught than taught when it comes to leadership in our homes. Howard Clark is one of the most polite, Godly, statesmen-like men I know. His son Jonathan's wife Emily wrote him a letter soon after the two of them were married, thanking Howard for teaching Jonathan to open the car door for her and treat her with thoughtfulness and kindness as a woman. Howard appreciated the letter, but told me later, "I never specifically instructed Jonathan to do that, but it has always been my practice with Kathy."

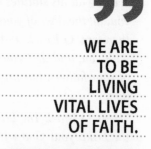

WE ARE TO BE LIVING VITAL LIVES OF FAITH.

We were with another family from the church at a community event when the 6-year-old son let loose with some vulgar language. The father looked our way and said, "I have no idea where he learned such language"—but we had an idea.

If we are going to lead our wife and family spiritually, we need to have a vital relationship with the Lord ourselves. I love the story about a grumpy old dad who was addressing his 16-year-old son in a somber, cheerless, and monotone speech: "Son, when I accepted Jesus, it was the most joyous day of my life. I have never had as much joy as I have today. I trust that someday you will have as much joy as a Christian as I do." What kid is going to want to sign up for that? If you truly have the joy of the Lord in your heart, would you mind notifying your face? This certainly does not mean we are to be laughing all the time, but we *are* to be living vital lives of faith.

Deuteronomy 6 is one of the most beloved passages in the Bible on how to raise children to love and follow the Lord. But count how many times those addressed as "you" are told to do something *themselves* before they are instructed to *"teach them diligently to your children."*

"Now this is the commandment—the statutes and the rules—that the LORD your God commanded me to teach you, that you may do them in the land to which you are going over, to possess it, that you may fear the LORD your God, you and your son and your son's son, by keeping all his statutes and his commandments, which I command you, all the days of your life, and that your days may be long. Hear therefore, O Israel, and be careful to do them, that it may go well with you, and that you may multiply greatly, as the LORD, the God of your fathers, has promised you, in a land flowing with milk and honey.

"Hear, O Israel: The LORD our God, the LORD is one. You shall love the LORD your God with all your heart and with all your soul and with all your might. And these words that I command you today shall be on your heart. You shall teach them diligently to your children, and shall talk of them when you sit in your house, and when you walk by the way, and when you lie down, and when you rise. You shall bind them as a sign on your hand, and they shall be as frontlets between your eyes. You shall write them on the doorposts of your house and on your gates." Deuteronomy 6:1–9

Years ago when the Promise Keepers movement was at its peak, a study was done on the effect of the husband's example spiritually. Here is what they found:

- When a child is the first to attend church, 3 1/2% of the time the family follows.
- When a wife/mom is the first to attend church, 17% of the time the family follows.
- When a husband/dad is the first to attend church, 93% of the time the family follows.

What an incredible affirmation of God's design for the husbands to be the spiritual leaders in the home. We *will* lead our family. The question is, "what direction will we lead?"

Your wife doesn't need you to have all the answers or to never sin. Your wife does need you to take spiritual initiative, demonstrating that the spiritual direction of the family is important to you.

FOUR SUGGESTIONS FOR DEVELOPING A DEEPER FAITH

- **Attend church regularly.**

If you want to learn to be like Jesus, you probably should check into His house more than two times a year. Hebrews 10:25 tells us not to neglect meeting together, but to encourage each other. For too many of us, we take the lead from our wife regarding church, secretly hoping that she will sleep in, or that she will suggest another option for Sunday. Even if our wife is not in town on Sunday, church is the place we should be. If you are not glad to go to church when you awaken on Sunday, you might want to look for a more vital church.

- **Have friends who love Jesus.**

Recently we were doing a study of Jesus healing the paralytic (see Mark 2:3–12). We talked about the fact that we are all paralyzed by something that keeps us from fully living as God designed us to—and that Jesus is the only one who can truly heal us. The question that really seemed to jump out was, "Who are your friends and where are they taking you?" Such a simple question, yet so important to ponder. Who are your best friends? Are they taking you *to* Jesus or *away* from Him? If the answer is "away from Him," then you can't have them as your best friends. Certainly you can be the friend that takes them *to* Jesus, but if they are taking you away from Him, you need to distance yourself.

- **Spend personal time with Jesus.**

Find something that works for you. Bible on audio, men's devotional guide, read through a book in the Bible each month, whatever. The book of Hebrews describes life as a race, saying:

> Let us also lay aside every weight, and sin which clings so closely, and let us run with endurance the race that is set before us, looking to Jesus, the founder and perfecter of our faith . . .   —Hebrews 12:1–2

In this race called life there are many weights and sins that encumber us and make us consider quitting. The writer says to run with endurance and look to Jesus, the One from whom we are getting our cues, our example, and our hope.

- **Make wise lifestyle decisions.**

A prominent pastor was caught in a hot tub with two topless women. When he was questioned, his defense was, "I cannot be held responsible for this immorality; I was drunk." We've gone a long way when our defense for our sinful actions is another sinful action.

Recall the four friends who carried the paralytic to Jesus and caused us to ask the question, "Who are your friends and where are they taking you?" We should also apply this question to our non-human "friends," by which I mean TV, movies, social media, alcohol, and so on.

The man of God who is going to lead his wife and family is a man who is making lifestyle decisions that help him live, as Ephesians 1:12 says, *"to the praise of His glory."*

YOU CAN'T BE JESUS, BUT YOU CAN LEAD YOUR FAMILY TO HIM

Barbara Boyd was one of the most humble, Godly women you would ever meet. She was engaged to Ralph Willoughby, a Godly young man, who suddenly became sick and died before Barbara and he were married. Barbara remained single and was the developer of the Bible and Life curriculum used by InterVarsity Christian Fellowship for many years. At Barbara's IVCF retirement party, she was given a spontaneous standing ovation by her admiring peers. After she quieted the crowd, she simply said, "When Jesus was riding into Jerusalem on the donkey, the donkey knew the applause was not for him. I am just a messenger and have had the privilege of carrying the message."

Your wife knows you are not Jesus. She isn't expecting you to lead just like He did, but she would love for you to be the donkey that brings the message of Jesus to your home.

A WORD FROM THE WIVES

Once again, the word that came up more than any other word was "initiative." It wasn't even always "leading," but initiating. It is amazing what a husband leading in prayer at the table or asking someone to pray will do for a family.

Here are wives' answers when asked to complete the sentence **"When it comes to our spiritual life, I would love it if ... "**

- "He led us in prayer together more often."

- "He initiated praying/reading scripture together more often, and led us as a family in churchgoing/events, including joining my co-ed Sunday School class (instead of having a conversation in the hallway with a friend or going home early)."

- "My husband would set aside time to pray with me each day."

- "He would initiate prayer and Bible study."

- "My husband took a stronger lead in setting the tone in our house. Specifically, incorporating family devotional/couples devotional time. As a wife, I feel that I handle so many things in the house, and this is one area where he really needs to take the lead. He says he wants to spend more time in the Word, but I need him to do something about it. Otherwise, I feel that I am expected to start it."

- "My husband asked to pray with me, took initiative, and read the Bible or devotional with our kids at the dinner table."

- "He would lead us in our growth together more. That he would be intentional about praying and pursuing God together. A Bible study with just the two of us for devotional purposes, not leadership purposes. I often feel very alone in my walk. He is a pastor and I sometimes feel as though I am the last one in the congregation to be ministered to."

- "He could control his alcohol consumption; I have a hard time accepting his level of spirituality when he comes home and the first thing he does is to prepare a drink."

- "My husband exceeds my expectations of being a spiritual leader in our family by leading us in family devotions every morning, pursuing ministry opportunities that our family can be a part of, and reading books and magazines to our girls that demonstrate his heart for them and for God. It truly is a beautiful thing."

CHAPTER HIGHLIGHTS

► Most couples struggle with their spiritual life together.

► Couples that pray regularly together have a divorce rate of less than 1%.

► Since prayer is so critical to vital Christian marriages, it's no wonder Satan does all he can to discourage it.

► Some thoughts about why praying together is so challenging:
  1. Differences in the way we communicate
  2. Temperament differences
  3. Differences in daily routines
  4. Different ways we grow spiritually
  5. Fear of being preached at

► Tips for praying together:
  1. Pick a specific time and make a commitment.
  2. Don't be upset if you miss a day.
  3. Decide who will do what.
  4. Set realistic expectations.
  5. Agree that neither one of you will preach in your praying.

► Before you can lead well, you must embrace your faith.

► When husbands lead, the family tends to follow.

► Four suggestions for developing a deeper faith with which to lead your family:
  1. Attend church regularly.
  2. Have friends who love Jesus.
  3. Spend personal time with Jesus.
  4. Make wise lifestyle decisions.

► Part of being the leader is to take the initiative to have Jesus be central in your home.

GAME PLAN

o Set up some strategy to personally read the Bible and pray for at least 5 minutes every day.

o Initiate a conversation with your spouse about some of the barriers to your praying together.

o Ask your wife if she would consider praying with you at some point every day.

o Talk about some suggestions in this chapter for helping the prayer times be more realistic.

o If you are a follower of Christ, take the initiative at each meal either to pray or to ask someone to pray.

o Look at the four suggestions for deepening your faith and commit to working on one of them in the next week.

TALKIN' WITH THE BROTHERS

1. How was spiritual leadership expressed, if it was, in your home?

2. What challenges to praying together affect you the most?
   - Differences in the way you communicate
   - Temperament differences
   - Differences in daily routines
   - Different ways you grow spiritually
   - Fear of being preached at

3. Any others you would add?

4. What have you found helpful in praying together?

5. What do you think of the "tips" proposed?
   - Pick a specific time and make a commitment.
   - Don't be upset if you miss a day.
   - Decide who will do what.
   - Set realistic expectations.
   - Agree that neither one of you will preach in your praying.

6. How did the Promise Keeper statistic on church attendance affect you?

7. Which of the four suggestions for deepening your faith do you find most challenging?

   - Attend church regularly.
   - Have friends who love Jesus.
   - Spend personal time with Jesus.
   - Make wise lifestyle decisions.

DISCUSSING THE WORD

⁴*"Hear, O Israel: The* LORD *our God, the* LORD *is one.* ⁵*You shall love the* LORD *your God with all your heart and with all your soul and with all your might.* ⁶*And these words that I command you today shall be on your heart.* ⁷*You shall teach them diligently to your children, and shall talk of them when you sit in your house, and when you walk by the way, and when you lie down, and when you rise.* ⁸*You shall bind them as a sign on your hand, and they shall be as frontlets between your eyes.* ⁹*You shall write them on the doorposts of your house and on your gates."*
                                                    —*Deuteronomy 6:4–9*

1. What strikes you about God's directives here?

2. What does He say is to take place before instructing the children in God's ways?

3. In what situations are we to "instruct" those around us? How widely should our commitment to the Lord be known?

9

Jesus Was Faithful to the Church

... but sometimes I just get so tired.

Steve Green* wrote a song years ago, "Find Us Faithful." The chorus goes like this:

> Oh may all who come behind us find us faithful
> May the fire of our devotion light their way
> May the footprints that we leave
> Lead them to believe
> And the lives we live inspire them to obey
> Oh may all who come behind us find us faithful
> Oh may all who come behind us find us faithful

PERFECT, NEVER . . . FAITHFUL, YES! I WANT TO DO THAT.

We husbands will be faced with challenges, and often we feel we can't do it perfectly, yet God calls us not to perfection but to faithfulness.

In the parable of the talents, the master uses the word "faithful" as the word to express his pleasure with his servants.

> "His master said to him, 'Well done, good and faithful servant. You have been faithful over a little; I will set you over much. Enter into the joy of your master.'"   —Matthew 25:21

---

* http://stevegreenministries.org/

When Paul writes to the church at Colossae he says,

To the saints and faithful brothers in Christ at Colossae: Grace to you and peace from God our Father. —Colossians 1:2

I love this. Paul didn't imply that the brothers in Colossae were without sin or never stumbled—but that they were faithful. This does not take away from the high call of Christlikeness, but it speaks of a heart desiring to follow after God.

> **GOD CALLS US NOT TO PERFECTION BUT TO FAITHFULNESS.**

We all come from various backgrounds and bring into our marriages a variety of challenges. God understands and does not expect the same from all of us—but He *does* call each of us to faithfulness. Our coach and mentor understands this will be a struggle at times, but He will be there for us.

. . . if we are faithless, he remains faithful— for he cannot deny himself. —2 Timothy 2:13

FAITHFUL TO PROVIDE

She sat in our office and shared that before marriage, her boyfriend had said that even though he had never held a job, he would get one after they were married. He even signed a paper promising it. After they married, her husband continued to sit at home all day watching TV and playing video games. In tears, she told us that before their first anniversary had arrived, they divorced. Because he didn't have a job, she had put the $25,000 for the wedding ceremony on her credit card. Not only was she devastated that her marriage lasted less than one year, she faced the sobering reality that she would be paying for the wedding for years to come. Well, she was not the sharpest knife in the drawer to marry a man who had never held a job, believing he would automatically become a hard-working provider after marriage, but nevertheless she had been taken. I went home from that counseling session and wrote our girls a letter: "I am glad your boyfriend is a Christian and plays the guitar, but does he have a job?" "No money, no honey" was my position.

WIRED TO PROVIDE

When Virginia and I were first married, my take-home salary was $600 a month and our house payment was $350 a month. Needless to say, we were not going out on the town much, except to garage sales. Occasionally I would come home and say, "Let's go out to dinner and a movie tonight." Virginia's response often was, "Love to, but we don't have enough money." She said it in a very matter-of-fact manner, with no sarcasm or meanness. The truth was simply that we had no money in our checking account. However, all I *heard* her say was "You are inept, and can't even supply us with enough money to go out on a date." There is something in the DNA of a man that is wired to be a provider. When we don't provide, most of us feel a bit emasculated. There are some men who seem to be okay with not working, but I am convinced most of them got discouraged somewhere along the way and their method of coping was to give up.

The apostle Paul is clear that a husband is to provide for his family:

But if anyone does not provide for his relatives, and especially for members of his household, he has denied the faith and is worse than an unbeliever. —*1 Timothy 5:8*

The responsibility to provide is clear, so let's talk about what that looks like.

First, it means that we are intentional in seeking work that will allow us to provide for our family. In times of financial distress, this may involve our spouse assisting or our taking a second job. This is a decision that you as a couple must make. It means you are to work in such a way that your *needs* are met—but not necessarily every desire that you, your wife, or your children have.

The operative word here is initiative. Most wives appreciate a hard-working man, even when they may not have an abundance of money. Take the initiative to talk as a couple about how you can better relieve the financial pressure in the family. Be willing to take a second job if necessary. Be faithful to the task of providing.

Second, seek a job that helps you come alive. Find others who are able to help you determine what job best suits your abilities and gifts. John Eldredge captures this well when he states:

> Don't ask yourself what the world needs. Ask yourself what makes you come alive, and go do that, because what the world needs is people who have come alive.
>
> —John Eldredge, *Wild at Heart*, p. 200

However, don't spend years waiting for a job that makes you "come alive" while your wife is working herself to death and you are not contributing to your family's finances. Be willing to work at Walmart or Starbucks as an hourly wage earner rather than waiting for the job "that meets your qualifications."

Third, don't offload this responsibility onto your wife, even if she can make more than you can. You need to be involved in the process of provision for the family. I realize there are situations that necessitate dads staying at home while the wife works, but we have seldom seen it end well. I am not saying that men are not able to nurture nor that women are not able to provide, but I am saying it seems clear from Genesis on that men are wired to protect and provide and woman are wired to nurture. Even the "curses" in Genesis 3 have to do with wiring. Regarding Adam, God says,

> *"Cursed is the ground because of you; in pain you shall eat of it all the days of your life; thorns and thistles it shall bring forth for you; and you shall eat the plants of the field. By the sweat of your face you shall eat bread . . ."*
> —Genesis 3:17–19

To Eve, God says,

> *"I will surely multiply your pain in childbearing; in pain you shall bring forth children."*
> —Genesis 3:16

Notice that work itself is not cursed, nor is childbearing, but the curses are related to what Adam and Eve were primarily designed to do in the Garden of Eden.

Fourth, lead your family in living within your means and being generous with what you have. The reason God says to bring your firstfruits to Him is that He deserves more than leftovers. Do you really need that cable package? Do you need to eat out for lunch at work? Is golf really a necessity? Make sure you are living within your means. Follow these four principles for finances and you will be well on your way to being a faithful leader in the area of finances:

1. Give to God.

   Honor the LORD with your wealth and with the firstfruits of all your produce. —*Proverbs 3:9*†

2. Give to yourself. Save 10% monthly. Establish your "Financial Freedom Fund."

   In the house of the wise are stores of choice food and oil, but a foolish man devours all he has. —*Proverbs 21:20 (NIV)*

3. Give to those to whom you owe. Pay your bills!

   Pay to all what is owed to them: taxes to whom taxes are owed, revenue to whom revenue is owed, respect to whom respect is owed, honor to whom honor is owed. Owe no one anything, except to love each other, for the one who loves another has fulfilled the law. —*Romans 13:7–8*

4. Give it away! Joyously! You will enjoy the use of money when you are free from the domination of money over your life.

   "In all things I have shown you that by working hard in this way we must help the weak and remember the words of the Lord Jesus, how he himself said, 'It is more blessed to give than to receive.'" —*Acts 20:35*

Fifth, take the initiative to make finances an area of prayer for the family. Make sure you are not always talking about your lack of money but failing to bring your needs to the Lord. Allow your children to see how God provides. Once, when I was a boy, our family didn't have enough money for food. Another family brought us a 100-pound bag of black-eyed beans. Now, that wasn't my first choice for lunch and

---

† See also: Matthew 23:23, Luke 11:42, Malachi 3:10

dinner, but with creativity my mom made a week's worth of meals out of that bag of beans, and we were thankful for God's provision.

Over the years our girls have seen God provide for them through generous friends offering vacation spots for our family, transportation vehicles when needed, clothes they no longer needed, and more. God has allowed us to be thankful for what He has provided rather than operate from a position of entitlement.

FAITHFUL SEXUALLY

Okay, huge area, and you might say, "But Jesus certainly was not tempted here, was He?" The scripture is plain that Jesus was fully God and fully man. The writer to the Hebrews says that Jesus was tempted "in every respect." Jesus did not allow His temptation to become sin, but He was fully man and fully tempted sexually.

For we do not have a high priest who is unable to sympathize with our weaknesses, but one who in every respect has been tempted as we are, yet without sin. —Hebrews 4:15

Most of our wives have no clue about the amount of temptation we face here. What makes it worse is that it was God who wired us to be sexually aroused visually, to be aroused quickly, and to think about sex frequently. When a wife gets undressed in front of her husband, he's aroused; when he gets undressed in front of her, she's "tired." Virginia and I will be watching TV and a somewhat provocative commercial comes on. Her response is, "Isn't that disgusting?" That wasn't the first thought that came through my mind. So her "helpful" suggestion to "just stop looking at those things" is not really helpful.

This has been a lifelong struggle for me from the day I picked up a sexually pornographic book on the side of the road in my teen years. I understand failure and struggle in this area. I also know what it is to have victory and I believe that without a plan, we will continually fail.

In this short section, there is not room to write much about this area, but I will encourage you to read some of the very helpful books published. *Every Man's Battle* and *Every Young Man's Battle* are very helpful resources. *Finally Free* by Heath Lambert is a great book on dealing with pornography.

What I will do here is give some very practical tips that have been helpful to me and many other men.

First, be in God's word daily. Pastor David Hegg puts it well when he states, "The only way to fight temptation is with an overwhelming desire for righteousness."

Second, surround yourself with God's people. Be in church regularly. Worship the Lord regularly and spend time with His people. They certainly are not perfect, but should make better friends and counselors than those who have no relationship with God. Have friends you really are honest with, who do more than "understand" your struggles. Have friends who are willing to hold your feet to the fire.

> **BE WILLING TO TAKE DRASTIC MEASURES TO AVOID A HABIT OF SINNING.**

Third, take drastic measures, if needed, to change your behavior. Many people dismiss Matthew 18:8–9 as not being literally true. It is literally true.

> *And if your hand or your foot causes you to sin, cut it off and throw it away. It is better for you to enter life crippled or lame than with two hands or two feet to be thrown into the eternal fire. And if your eye causes you to sin, tear it out and throw it away. It is better for you to enter life with one eye than with two eyes to be thrown into the hell of fire.*
> —Matthew 18:8–9

It is indeed better to go into heaven physically maimed than to go to hell physically whole. We do realize, especially in the area of sexual temptation, that plucking out an eye or cutting off an appendage will not keep you from sinning. What Jesus is saying is to be willing to take drastic measures to avoid a habit of sinning.

I had a youth pastor friend who was struggling with masturbation. He thought he was the only pastor who struggled with this. Wrong! He would come to me and share, "I failed again." Obviously my hearing his failure was not motivation enough to change. I used a parenting principle with this young man that we used with our children. "The displeasure of the discipline must exceed the pleasure of the disobedience." Telling me obviously didn't do the trick. So I told him that every time he looked at pornography and or masturbated, I would tell his wife—that stopped it! Have guys who love you enough to be tough enough to help. If we are honest, many of us want to cut back on our sexual sin, but not eliminate it.

> **I HAVE NEVER MET A MAN WHO SAYS, "SETTING BOUNDARIES ON MY RELATIONSHIPS HAS REALLY HURT MY MARRIAGE."**

An example in my own life came when we changed cable providers. The new provider included HBO and Cinemax for free for the first 3 months. What I found as I "surfed" the stations was that I stayed in the "harmful surf" too long. The next day I called the cable provider and asked them to cancel HBO and Cinemax on our TV. We had an interesting discussion as he tried to explain there was no reason to cancel since we were not paying for it. Only after I finally said, "I want those movie channels off my TV or I will cancel our service with you" did they do as I asked. The reason I did that was that I know I can be strong *many* nights at 11 or 12, but not *every* night, especially when I feel unsatisfied or rejected by my wife. I don't know what your drastic measures are, but you do. Perhaps it's not getting coffee at the convenience store that has sexually explicit magazines displayed. Perhaps it's not watching TV alone. Perhaps it's putting a system on your computer so another person is notified of every website you look at. An excellent resource is found at www.xxxchurch.com (make sure you put "church" after "xxx").

It is important to understand the difference between temptation and sin. Someone once said, "You can't stop the birds from flying over your head, but you can keep them from building a nest in your hair." I often told the college men at our summer camp on Catalina

Island that when they walked down the street in the tourist town of Avalon, they might see scantly clad women walking toward them— that's temptation. But running into a post while staring at them— that's sin. The apostle Paul wrote:

> *No temptation has overtaken you that is not common to man. God is faithful, and he will not let you be tempted beyond your ability, but with the temptation he will also provide the way of escape, that you may be able to endure it.* —*1 Corinthians 10:13*

God will provide a way of escape for us; our responsibility is to use it.

Fourth, don't have an affair! It sounds so simple, right? Not to the thousands of men who find themselves ensnared in infidelity. "I don't know how it happened," he said, sitting in our counseling office. Pardon me, but he did know how it happened. He started talking with her more than other employees, complimenting her, meeting her to go over papers, "happening" to come in to work on Saturdays when she mentioned she'd be there, sharing about his disappointment in marriage. He knew, and he didn't do anything about it. Gentlemen, if you ever start enjoying being in the presence of someone of the opposite sex other than your wife, and look forward to seeing this person, you need to curtail or end the association. The destruction of an affair is cataclysmic. Don't do it.

Men, don't ride in cars alone with another woman, don't eat with a woman alone, don't keep any secrets from your wife, don't talk with another woman about your marital issues, don't strike up a Facebook conversation with another woman, and don't have any accounts your wife does not share or have passwords to access. I realize these are a lot of "don'ts," but I can tell you this: I have never met a man who says, "Setting boundaries on my relationships has really hurt my marriage." Scripture says that there should not be even a hint of sexual immorality.

Let such a relationship play out fully in your mind. What will it be like when your wife finds out? How will your children respond when you tell them you are leaving them for another woman? What will this do to your work relationships? Church involvement?

A man who was having an affair with a babysitter told me he didn't know what to do as he didn't want to hurt anyone's feelings. I told him, "That train has left." I also asked him, "How did you expect this to play out? Did you see it ending well?"

Fifth, and I know this is somewhat offensive to many: watch your alcohol intake. Too many men have compromised themselves relationally after becoming "less inhibited" by alcohol. I find it hard enough to avoid sin when fully inhibited; I certainly don't need to be less inhibited.

Now, drinking a glass of wine with dinner or a beer with your burger is not a sin. After all, Jesus drank wine. So the issue is not "can you drink?" but "should you drink?" Scripture is clear, however, about being drunk or mastered by anything: don't let it happen. "Free in Christ" does not mean "free to sin."

For those of you who have children, the studies on date rape and alcohol are staggering. More than 80% of date rape is alcohol-related.‡ I have a great concern for our youth who see their dads drinking (and perhaps even abusing) alcohol. They think this gives them license to drink themselves. Unfortunately, they often have less self-control regarding alcohol than their adult counterparts.

Being found faithful is a high calling and not always an easy one, but it is encouraging to me that in the parable of the faithful servants, the master says to them, *"You have been faithful over a little; I will set you over much. Enter into the joy of your master."* (Matthew 25:23) Somehow when we set our minds on habitually being faithful in the "little" choices we make, the larger ones will not seem as difficult.

FAITHFUL WHEN REJECTED

Many of us grew up in homes where we would be promised something if we did something else. *If* you are good in church, we will go to McDonald's on the way home. *If* you clean your plate, you will get dessert. So we may expect in marriage that if we do something for our wife, we will be rewarded.

---

‡   https://healthresearchfunding.org/39-date-rape-statistics-college-campuses

Most of us believe, "If I do something for her, she should do something for me. If she doesn't do something for me, I am off the hook for doing something for her." But we are told to love our wives *"as Christ loved the Church,"* **period**—not *"if* they are treating us as we wish." The apostle Paul instructs husbands to love their wives, and he doesn't include the disclaimer "unless she is sick" or "unless she has a headache" or "unless she isn't treating you with respect" or "unless she fails to take care of herself." He simply says, *"Husbands, love your wives, as Christ loved the Church . . ."* (Ephesians 5:25).

Now, think about that for a moment. How did the Church respond to Christ? Many deserted Him, some denied Him; ultimately they left him to die alone. Fortunately, His love for us is not dependent on our response to Him. Again, Paul states, *"If we are faithless, he remains faithful— for he cannot deny himself."* (2 Timothy 2:13)

There may be seasons of our marriage or situations in our marriage during which we are simply called to be faithful to our marriage out of our love for the Lord. I recently received an email from a man married to an extremely controlling and negative wife:

> My marriage is still intact. I have adopted the mindset that to the best of my ability, I'm going to honor and obey God in all my thoughts, words, and actions in my marriage, regardless of what my wife does or says. It is not easy! And it is less than wonderful a lot of times, but I am determined to honor God, and keep at it and wait for Him to work in me and my marriage.

WHAT A MAN!

I was riding in the car with a friend one day when he said, "I bet I am the only 40-year-old married virgin you have met." Knowing he had been married for 15 years, I assumed Virginia was right and I really did need to have my hearing checked. I was unsure what to say, so being a regular sort of guy, I said nothing.

A few days later, I got up my courage and said, "I may have heard you wrong, but I thought you said something about being a 40-year-old virgin."

"You heard correctly. My wife and I have never fully consummated our marriage through sexual intercourse. She was sexually molested earlier in life and is still working through that with a therapist. We do connect sexually—she has been good about making every effort—but we have yet to experience the sexual relationship fully."

As I drove home that day I said out loud in the car, "What a man!" In a culture where men often judge their masculinity by their sexual conquests, my friend was a real man by honoring, loving, and serving God and his wife.

PUT TO DEATH SOME EXPECTATIONS

There are times we need to put to death some of our dreams and expectations that cannot or likely will not be met in our spouse. Perhaps we married someone we loved running with and because of an injury she no longer is able to run. Or perhaps we married someone who was sleek and slender, but bearing children has not been kind to her body. I remember a couple where the wife was an avid surfer and married a man who was not. She fully expected him to not only learn, but grow to love surfing. He didn't, and eventually she left him for someone who did.

Sometimes we just need to realize, "not with this wife." As much as Virginia loves me, I have put to death the idea that she is going to grow to love being in a jacuzzi with me. I don't ask or expect that ever to happen, because that dream has been put to death. Let me assure you, she has put to death a whole lot more dreams that she had about a husband for the sake of our marriage, such as that I will ever repair anything. It costs more to repair an item after I have worked on it than before I have touched it. It is a whole lot more beneficial spending our time celebrating what we do have in each other rather than complaining about what we don't have.

A WORD FROM THE WIVES

It should not come as a surprise, but when we are not faithful in the areas of alcohol and sexual purity, it is especially hard on our wives. These are big areas, but not at all impossible to deal with and to be faithful in.

Here are wives' answers when asked to complete the sentence **"The biggest challenge to our marriage has been . . ."**

- "My husband's addiction to porn—it warped his mind and damaged our family in more ways then I can share. However by loving, forgiving, and lots of help and counsel, our family is very loving and functional."

- "An affair that he had a couple of years ago. It's not necessarily the affair itself, but the feelings of not trusting, questioning everything and everyone. It's hard to get through the affair and even harder to push through reminders and mistrusts."

- "His trouble with reading about sex online. It hurts him, and it hurts me. It makes me feel like I'm not enough for him."

- "On his travel for work he is confronted with a lot of 'soft pornography' which is really hard for him to resist. Especially when he is already feeling lonely and pressured by the work demands."

- "My husband's extramarital affair."

- "He had an affair (emotional). That makes it worse because he liked her, not just her body."

- "Infidelity and everything that comes along with it."

- "Not being truthful about his temptation addiction to homosexual pornography."

- "We have been married for 38 years in December. Alcoholism was most damaging the first 13 years."

CHAPTER HIGHLIGHTS

► God has called us to provide for our families financially.

► God has called us to sexual purity in mind and deed.

► Maintaining sexual purity often requires drastic actions.

► God will provide a way for us to escape temptation.

► Our motivation to love our wife well should not be based on her response.

► Jesus set the example of loving those who often did not love in response.

► The truest love is loving even when we know our spouse will not be able to reciprocate.

► The ultimate joy for us is in knowing we are doing what Jesus desires.

GAME PLAN

o Take the lead to sit down with your wife to work out a budget together, or connect with a third party who can help you in this area.

o Take radical steps to eliminate the areas you are most frequently tempted in sexually.

o Each morning this week, ask your wife what you can do for her.

o If your wife treats you poorly, don't respond in anger, but look for ways to do something nice for her.

o Look for ways to serve her this week when she can't "pay you back." For instance, do the dishes or clean up a room, even if you are not going to be home later to hear her response.

TALKIN' WITH THE BROTHERS

1. What are the greatest challenges for you in providing for your family?

2. What have you found to be the most helpful strategy or practice in the battle of sexual purity?

3. What are some ways we are tempted to base our expressions of love for our wife on her response to us?

4. Why do you think Jesus continued to the cross after His followers all deserted Him?

5. Share, if you wish, a time in your marriage where you continued to love your wife through a difficult time.

6. What have the results been when you have loved your wife like Christ, even when you ain't no Jesus?

DISCUSSING THE WORD

¹Now Joseph had been brought down to Egypt, and Potiphar, an officer of Pharaoh, the captain of the guard, an Egyptian, had bought him from the Ishmaelites who had brought him down there. ²The LORD was with Joseph, and he became a successful man, and he was in the house of his Egyptian master. ³His master saw that the LORD was with him and that the LORD caused all that he did to succeed in his hands. ⁴So Joseph found favor in his sight and attended him, and he made him overseer of his house and put him in charge of all that he had. ⁵From the time that he made him overseer in his house and over all that he had, the LORD blessed the Egyptian's house for Joseph's sake; the blessing of the LORD was on all that he had, in house and field. ⁶So he left all that he had in Joseph's charge, and because of him he had no concern about anything but the food he ate.

Now Joseph was handsome in form and appearance. ⁷And after a time his master's wife cast her eyes on Joseph and said, "Lie with me." ⁸But he refused and said to his master's wife, "Behold, because of me my master has no concern about anything in the house, and he has put everything that he has in my charge. ⁹He is not greater in this house than I am, nor has he kept back anything from me except you, because you are his wife. How then can I do this great wickedness and sin against God?" ¹⁰And as she spoke to Joseph day after day, he would not listen to her, to lie beside her or to be with her.

¹¹But one day, when he went into the house to do his work and none of the men of the house was there in the house, ¹²she caught him by his garment, saying, "Lie with me." But he left his garment in her hand and fled and got out of the house. ¹³And as soon as she saw that he had left his garment in her hand and had fled out of the house, ¹⁴she called to the men of her household and said to them, "See, he has brought among us a Hebrew to laugh at us. He came in to me to lie with me, and I cried

149

out with a loud voice. *[15]And as soon as he heard that I lifted up my voice and cried out, he left his garment beside me and fled and got out of the house." [16]Then she laid up his garment by her until his master came home, [17]and she told him the same story, saying, "The Hebrew servant, whom you have brought among us, came in to me to laugh at me. [18]But as soon as I lifted up my voice and cried, he left his garment beside me and fled out of the house."*

[19]As soon as his master heard the words that his wife spoke to him, "This is the way your servant treated me," his anger was kindled. [20]And Joseph's master took him and put him into the prison, the place where the king's prisoners were confined, and he was there in prison. [21]But the LORD *was with Joseph and showed him steadfast love and gave him favor in the sight of the keeper of the prison. [22]And the keeper of the prison put Joseph in charge of all the prisoners who were in the prison. Whatever was done there, he was the one who did it. [23]The keeper of the prison paid no attention to anything that was in Joseph's charge, because the* LORD *was with him. And whatever he did, the* LORD *made it succeed.*   —Genesis 39

1. What repeated phrase in this chapter jumps out for you?

2. What strikes you most about Joseph in this account?

3. Do you think Potiphar believed his wife's story? Why or why not?

4. What situations are you in that challenge your faithfulness in following the Lord?

5. What principles or examples from Joseph's life encourage you?

10

Jesus Left a Legacy of Joy

I want to do that, too.

ONE LEGO AT A TIME

As I was watching a Boston Red Sox game a few years ago, a 6-foot-7-inch replica of David Ortiz, "Big Papi," was unveiled at Fenway Park. What caught my attention about this statue was that it was made of Lego blocks—34,510 of them, taking 290 man-hours to construct. The finished product was spectacular, but what was more amazing was the realization that the process was accomplished one Lego piece at a time.

Loving our wives is not rocket science, but it is time-consuming and it is done one small step at a time. Few of us can take our wives on a round-the-world cruise, or buy her a 5-carat diamond or a BMW convertible, but we can take out the trash, tell her how nice she looks, take a walk with her, and listen while she tells us in detail about her day. It is the little things that make up for the big memories.

I trust as you have read and discussed these pages you have been encouraged to do the little things that demonstrate your big heart. Yesterday, Virginia and I returned from a ten-day trip. I was leaving to run an errand in one car and I knew she was going to leave soon for an errand she had to run. It may not seem like a big thing, but I started her car to make sure it would start, ran the windshield washers to wash off the dust that had settled in our absence, and pulled the car away from the tree it was parked close to so she could get in more easily. I don't mean to pat myself on the back (okay, I guess I did), but these are the types of little things that say, "I love you." I contrast that with our neighbor who, after a foot of snow had fallen overnight, scraped the snow off his car and drove off, leaving his wife to scrape the snow off her own car before she went to work. It's the little things that say, "I am thinking of you and want you to know I love you, even when you are not watching or sometimes are not even aware."

ONE GENERATION AWAY

Some of you have come from families of origin that did not model Christ-like love in any form. You may be discouraged, thinking, "I wish I had had that model." May I encourage you to sidle up to another man you look up to as a Godly husband or Godly dad, and ask him out for a meal. Don't ask him to mentor you—it will freak him out—just ask him some questions you might have about life as a man.

You see, you are only one generation away from changing your family legacy. I will never forget the December gathering where, as we were sharing our Christmas traditions, a young NFL player holding his six-week-old son said, with tears, "I wish I had grown up in your family. We never had any Christmas traditions, let alone Christ-centered ones." Virginia immediately responded, "But just think, when your son is a young adult, he can say, 'Oh, yes, our family always had Christ-centered traditions. I am so blessed to have been raised in such a family.'" You may not have had a Christ-centered marriage and family modeled for you, but your wife and children can have a Christ-centered marriage and family experience.

DO THE "I WISH I HAD" NOW

Virginia and I told this story in our book *The Marriage App*, but I think it bears repeating:

It was John and Wendy's favorite vacation spot during their 38-year marriage: twice each year they would fly to Hawaii and rent a cottage or stay in a timeshare, sometimes alone, but often with their family. The islands held many memories for them of a life well-spent, a close family, and a sweet marriage. But after a 17-year battle with cancer, John lost his earthly struggle and entered his heavenly rest. Wendy had asked us to accompany her on her first return visit to Hawaii after John's death. We were having lunch out on the balcony overlooking the Pacific when Wendy started to cry. Assuming she was recalling some special time on the island with John, we gently asked her, "What is it, Wendy?" She blurted out, "I wish I'd made him more Jell-O!"

Wendy then told us, through laughter and tears, that John loved Jell-O. From the earliest days of their marriage, John always was asking her to make him Jell-O. She didn't like Jell-O herself and declined to make it most of the time, claiming it was all empty calories, nothing but sugar and colored dyes. But now, looking back, she mused, "Why didn't I just give him Jell-O?" As we continued to talk, she said, "The real reason was not all the nutritional stuff, but just that I plain didn't want to make him Jell-O. I didn't like it. But what a simple thing for me to do to bring him a little extra joy for the day. I wish I had made him more Jell-O."

Fortunately, in John and Wendy's case, there were not a lot of other "Jell-O" areas. Unfortunately, for many couples, the accumulation of "Jell-O" moments—not caring about our spouse's needs and desires—culminates in individuals not feeling cared for and loved. In too many cases those marriages end in divorce, or continue in a silent state of contempt and miss out on the joy of intimacy in marriage.

What are some of the potential "I wish I would haves" in your marriage? How about doing them now?

TAKE THE INITIATIVE TO CREATE MEMORIES THAT WILL LAST A LIFETIME

One older widow, responding to the survey question: "The best time we ever had as a couple . . ." wrote,

> The time a work friend let us use his home on a lovely small lake in the middle of the week without our children. No one was in the cabins nearby, so we had complete privacy. We had sex on the raft, on a blanket on a tiny island in a wooded area, on the living room couch, and on a waterbed—for the first time ever—and we walked around the house and deck naked. It was more romantic than our honeymoon. We enjoyed complete privacy and intimate lovemaking and conversation. It was the best week in my memory that I will forever cherish.

Another wife wrote:

> This Wednesday was my birthday. I came out to the kitchen as usual in the dark and turned on the light to find the entire kitchen covered with post-it notes from my husband, spelling out messages of love and affirmation. After I read each one, through tears, I took a bunch of pictures and a video. There were a bunch of roses, too. What a difference from 5 years ago!!! One of the reasons it was sooo special was that he demonstrated that he knows me (one of the messages, in fact, was: "I know you") which makes me feel very loved and that he's listened to me. I've had a hip and back injury that has really slowed me down this year and completely stopped my workout routine, so I've made comments like, "old woman walking" and told him how it has gotten me down to be so inactive and to feel so frail and in pain. So he wrote a theme of "You are . . ." and wrote "you are loved, young, strong, special, a blessing, sexy, great person, beautiful, smart," etc. After a bit, he woke up and came out to the kitchen and I couldn't stop hugging him. The best birthday

present ever. So then I took him back to bed and he said it seemed like it was *his* birthday! :) To be treasured this much by my husband was beyond my wildest dreams.

Often, a little initiative and creativity can create a memory that will last a lifetime.

LOVE HER WELL AND WATCH HER CHANGE

The story is told of a man wanting to divorce his wife and hurt her as much as possible. He went to a divorce lawyer and asked him how they could make the divorce as painful as possible for his wife. The lawyer started by asking the man if his wife also wanted the divorce. "Absolutely," he replied, "she hates my guts."

The lawyer said, "The divorce will actually give your wife what she wants. Here is my suggestion. For the next month, cater to your wife's every need and desire. If she loves flowers, bring her flowers. Listen to her as she talks, and ask follow-up questions as though you were really interested in her. Help with the dishes, and surprise her if she is out for some period of time by doing some chores. In other words, try to get her to fall in love with you again. At the end of the month, after she has fallen for you, divorce her. *That* will hurt her."

"Sounds great," responded the client, "I'm in."

A month passed and the lawyer noticed he had not received a call back from his client. So he called to ask if the client was ready to file divorce papers.

"Why?" asked the husband, "we have a great marriage. We don't want to get a divorce."

We counseled a couple once where the husband was leaving the wife because she was "so critical of me, nags me, and doesn't seem to trust me." You might start feeling sorry for the man until you hear "the rest of the story." He impregnated her before they were married and had had multiple affairs after they were married. He was really into himself and his own success. I have often wondered how different his wife would have been if she had been well loved.

When I think of how love can change a woman, I think of the story of "The Eight-Cow Wife," set on the fictional Pacific islands of Kiniwata and Narabundi. The story is about a man who came to Kiniwata in search of a good fishing guide. Everyone recommended a young man from Narabundi named Johnny Lingo, but then started laughing. When the visitor asked why they were laughing, he was told of how Johnny Lingo paid eight cows for Sam Karoo's daughter, Sarita. The visitor knew enough about island customs to know that eight cows was a tremendously high price, so he commented that Sarita must be gorgeous. He knew that three cows would fetch a decent wife, and five, a beauty.

The locals explained that it was so funny because Sarita would be called "plain" at best. Most thought she was homely and knew her father, Sam Karoo, was hoping for two cows but would settle for one for his daughter.

When the visitor finally met Johnny Lingo in his home on Narabundi, he became even more confused. We pick up the story in detail here:

> And then I saw her. Through the glass-beaded portieres that shimmered in the archway, I watched her enter the adjoining room to place a bowl of blossoms on the dining table. She was the most beautiful woman I have ever seen. The lift of her shoulders, the tilt of her chin, the sparkle of her eyes all spelled a pride to which no one could deny her the right.
>
> I turned back to Johnny and found him looking at me. "You admire her?" he murmured.
>
> "She—she's glorious," I said. "Who is she?"
>
> "That is Sarita."
>
> "But she's not the Sarita from Kiniwata." I said.
>
> "There is only one Sarita. Perhaps you wish to say she does not look the way they say she looked in Kiniwata."
>
> "She doesn't." The impact of her appearance made me forget tact. "I heard she was homely, or at least nondescript. They all make fun of you because you let yourself be cheated by Sam Karoo."
>
> "You think he cheated me? You think eight cows were too many?" A smile slid over his lips as I shook my head.

"But I don't understand. How can she be so different from the way she was described?"

"Do you ever think," he asked reflectively, "what it must mean to a woman to know that her husband has met with her father to settle the lowest price for which she can be bought? And then later, when all the women talk, they boast of what their husbands paid for them. One says four cows, another maybe six. How does she feel, the woman who was sold for one or two? This could not happen to my Sarita."

"Then you paid that unprecedented number of cows just to make your wife happy?"

"I wanted Sarita to be happy, yes, but I wanted more than that. You say she's different from the way they remember her in Kiniwata. This is true. Many things can change a woman. Things that happen inside, things that happen outside. But the thing that matters most is what she thinks about herself. In Kiniwata, Sarita believed she was worth nothing. Now she knows she is worth more than any other woman on the islands."

"Then you wanted—"

"I wanted to marry Sarita. I loved her and no other woman. But," he finished softly, "I wanted an eight-cow wife." *

What sort of wife do you want? How have you helped her know how precious she is to you? In Ephesians 5:27, Jesus is the model for our call to help our wives become more radiant. Is your wife becoming more radiant as you love her well and encourage her to become all God has gifted her to be? Truth be told, many of our wives are looking a bit haggard because they have devoted themselves to helping *our* dreams come true. Let's use our authority in the home to help them realize more of *their* dreams. As we do this, I think we, too, will turn out to have "eight-cow" wives. (By the way, if you're anywhere but Kiniwata, best not to ever use the word "cow" when talking to or describing your wife.)

---

* excerpted and condensed from "Johnny Lingo and the Eight-Cow Wife" by Patricia McGerr, published in Woman's Day, Curtis Brown, Ltd., November 1965.

EXPECTATION OF JOY

There certainly are no guarantees, but often when we lead and love well, our wives will respond in ways we had always hoped they would. The book of Hebrews describes Jesus as:

> . . . *the founder and perfecter of our faith, who for the joy that was set before him endured the cross, despising the shame, and is seated at the right hand of the throne of God.*   —*Hebrews 12:2*

Sometimes we are simply called to obey, because we are doing something far bigger than "just for us." Certainly the joy set before Jesus was reuniting with the Father, but He also was to have the joy of knowing that He accomplished what He was called to do.

Not to over-spiritualize this too much, but when we unselfishly serve our spouse and do things that are sacrificial, it may be tiring, boring, exhausting, or painful in the moment, but there is joy afterwards in knowing that we did "what we were meant to do." In the words of the theologian, New England Patriots coach Bill Belichick, "Do your job!" It also strikes me that, just as Jesus' sacrifice allowed Him to have the joy of being reunited with the Father, so our sacrifice for our wives often reunites us with them in the relationship God intended.

Final Thoughts

TRUST GOD AND SEE HOW GOOD HE IS

For many years my family and I were involved in a camp on Catalina Island called Campus By the Sea. Until recently, the island had a huge herd of wild pigs. Our practice was to feed the pigs three times a day with all the leftover food not eaten by the campers. One of my responsibilities as a college-age staff member was to drive the water-skiing boat each morning at 6 am. Inevitably, as I headed to the boats, I encountered a trash can that had been turned over by some pigs the night before, with trash strewn everywhere. As I picked up the trash, I thought, "You stupid pigs, we feed you a banquet three times a day, and yet you rummage through the trash hoping for a tasty morsel." Then it was about as close to an audible voice I have ever heard from God saying, "Who is the stupid one? I have given you everything you could need in life and more, and yet you still feel the need to rummage around in sinful trash choices, hoping for a tantalizing morsel." So true, so sad.

There is a passage in scripture that says, *"Oh, taste and see that the Lord is good!"* (Psalm 34:8) I trust that you will be willing to "taste" what God has for you in you life and marriage. It actually is quite good.

USE YOUR MARRIAGE FOR KINGDOM PURPOSES

Men, your wife knows you ain't no Jesus. But when she sees you striving to be more like Jesus, I believe she will be drawn more fully to you. When you and your wife love each other well, your children will notice and be drawn to the One who supplies all you need to love. When our families honor each other and the Lord, people will notice.

Virginia and I were invited to speak in Hawaii a few years ago. (Our response to the invitation was, "Here I am Lord, send me"!) While there, we found a lagoon teeming with turtles. We swam with them and took pictures of them, and then eagerly shared our photos upon our return to the mainland. Every time we showed the pictures, the response was the same: "Where is that? We want to experience that ourselves."

May God grant us the courage and delight to live in such a way that people say, "I want a marriage like yours. I want a family like yours." Then we can point them to the One who makes this possible. The world desperately wants to know if the Gospel is real. Does following Christ really make a difference? What an incredible honor to love our wives well and in the process point people to Christ, even when we ain't no Jesus.

A Legacy Left

Once upon a time there were two people who thought they had a pretty good marriage even though they argued and hurt each other a good bit. The couple met a mature couple and thought, "Their marriage looks really good and fun—not like anything we've seen before." They hung out with them whenever they could. The older couple invited them to a marriage retreat and, coming home, the husband accepted Christ. Everything changed for them. Every aspect of their lives has been transformed. And *now* they have a marriage that's not perfect but so good that they don't even recognize themselves at times. It's also unlike anything their family members and friends who don't know Christ have seen before and they notice. God gets *all* the glory.

We are that couple and you can be as well. Because even though you ain't no Jesus—He is, and He is all you need.

—Amy and Ken Gaudet
Massachusetts

A WORD FROM THE WIVES

Leaving a legacy is established not after death, but by actions now that have lasting effects as people observe your marriage.

Here are wives' answers when asked to complete the sentence **"I wish just once my husband would . . ."**

- "Take me out on an impromptu date to *anywhere*."
- "Share his feelings about a personal matter in his heart or our marriage."
- "Write me love notes and leave them for me throughout my day."
- "Plan our dates. He's only planned one since we married."
- "I wish, just once, my husband would compliment me or encourage me for who I am and for how I am as a wife, friend, mother, and ministry leader/speaker."

CHAPTER HIGHLIGHTS

▶ Just as when building a Lego structure, loving our wives well is done one small deed at a time.

▶ No matter what our background, we are only one generation away from a Godly legacy.

▶ Some day one of you will pass away and the other will say, "I wish we had . . ." Why not do those things now?

▶ Take the time and resources now to create memories that will last a lifetime.

▶ When you love your wife well, there is a good chance she will become the woman you always dreamed of.

▶ Use your marriage as a witness to the power of the Gospel to transform lives and give "life to the full."

GAME PLAN

o Ask your wife if the two of you could set aside some time to talk about what your highest goals are for your marriage and family.

o Think about what your wife often says she wishes you would do more, and do it this week.

o Plan something that will create a memory for the two of you. Go away to a special place for a weekend.

o Get rid of the kids and have a meal in front of the fireplace prepared (or ordered) by you.

o Talk about ways you can be an example to those around you of what a Christ-centered marriage can be.

o Give your wife your "review" of this book and let her read the bonus chapter, written especially for her.

TALKIN' WITH THE BROTHERS

1. Talk about some of the seemingly "small" things you have done for your wife in the past weeks that have made a difference in your relationship.

2. What are some "I wish I had" moments you could create now?

3. What experiences could you initiate that would be memory makers for you as a couple?

4. Tell of someone noticing the state of your marriage and asking you about it.

5. Share with each other your greatest "takeaway" from your weeks together studying how to love your wives like Christ.

DISCUSSING THE WORD

[14]"Now fear the Lord and serve him with all faithfulness. Throw away the gods your ancestors worshiped beyond the Euphrates River and in Egypt, and serve the Lord. [15]But if serving the Lord seems undesirable to you, then choose for yourselves this day whom you will serve, whether the gods your ancestors served beyond the Euphrates, or the gods of the Amorites, in whose land you are living. But as for me and my household, we will serve the Lord." —Joshua 24:14–15 (NIV)

1. What are the "gods" our forefathers may have worshiped or that we might be tempted to worship today?

2. What watershed decision affects our legacy more than anything?

3. What does *"as for me and my household, we will serve the Lord"* look like for you as you lead your household and leave a legacy for the next generation?

Bonus

Ladies, if you are reading the book, a few thoughts for you . . .

It is no secret that women tend to read more books on relationships than their husbands. Many wives buy books for their husbands and put them on their nightstand to "encourage" them to read. (Some of them are so helpful that they highlight the parts they feel their husbands really need to read.) I am making the assumption that many of you have picked up this book with the hopes that your husband will read it and love you more "like Christ." Others of you have picked it up with some curiosity as to what husbands are being encouraged to do, just to make sure the author got it right.

Whatever the reason, I trust these few thoughts will be an encouragement to you and maybe even a bit enlightening on how to better help your husband love you like Christ, even when he ain't no Jesus.

He is different by design—God's design.

It was not good for Adam to be alone, so God made a suitable partner for him to complement, not duplicate, him—*you*! Scripture says:

> *The LORD God said, "It is not good for the man to be alone. I will make a helper suitable for him."* —*Genesis 2:18 (NIV)*

"Helper suitable" or "helper fit for him," in the Hebrew, written "ēzer k'negdŏ," literally means someone "like, but like-opposite." *Like*, because you both are equal and bear the image of God, but *opposite* in that by design you were made to complement, not duplicate, each other.

BEING MADE IN THE IMAGE OF GOD AS A MAN IS VERY DIFFERENT FROM BEING MADE IN THE IMAGE OF GOD AS A WOMAN.

May I encourage you to realize that being made in the image of God as a man is very different from being made in the image of God as a woman. Instead of trying to make him more like you, I would suggest you look for ways to appreciate his maleness or "opposite-ness." Try as you may, most men will not likely suddenly love quiche, *Pride and Prejudice*, spending Super Bowl weekend at a quaint bed and breakfast that has no TV, or a dollop of anything. He will likely continue to grunt, not take appearance as seriously as you do, pick his nose, and leave his clothes on the bedroom floor. This does not make him bad, just different. We are not talking about areas of sin. Being a man is never an excuse for sinful actions or thoughts. But preferences are often not moral issues, they are just that—preferences.

If you were going to a hardware store to get two fittings to join two pieces of hose together, you would ask for "a male and a female" adapter. The difference in the two makes the connection strong and allows water to flow through it. So it is in marriage: when we appreciate our differences, it actually makes us stronger, more useful, and better together.

Instead of saying something like "You make no sense to me," say, "Wow, I never would have thought about it that way. Would you explain that more fully to me?" Instead of saying, with a tone, "What's wrong with you? Why did you do that?" say, "Wow, we are so different in the way we do things."

We are living in a day where gender differences are being minimized. This is not new; Robert Bly wrote about the effects of this phenomenon years ago:

> In the seventies I began to see all over the country a phenomenon that we might call the "soft male." Sometimes even today when I look out at an audience, perhaps half the young males are what I'd call soft. They're lovely, valuable people—I like them—they're not interested in harming the earth or starting wars. There's a gentle attitude toward life in their whole being and style of living.
>
> But many of these men are not happy. You quickly notice the lack of energy in them. They are life-preserving but not exactly life-giving.   —Robert Bly, *Iron John*, p. 3

More recently, John Eldredge wrote about this in his wonderful book *Wild at Heart*, commenting on the effect of a young boy being raised primarily by a mom and the lack of a father's influence in a boy's life.

> Femininity can never bestow masculinity. My mother would often call me "sweetheart," but my father called me "tiger."
>
> A classic example of these dueling roles took place the other night. We were driving down the road and the boys were talking about the kind of car they want to get when it comes time for their first set of wheels. "I was thinking about a Humvee, or a motorcycle, maybe even a tank. What do you think, Dad?" "I'd go with the Humvee. We could mount a machine gun on top." "What about you, Mom— what kind of car do you want me to have?" You know what she said . . . "A safe one."
>
> Her first reaction—"a safe one"—is so natural, so understandable. After all, she is the incarnation of God's tenderness. But if a mother will not allow her son to become dangerous, if she does not let the father take him away, she will emasculate him.
>
> —John Eldredge, *Wild At Heart*, pp. 64–65

There is a reason God created us male and female. By design God wanted the *two* to become one. God designed you to function best as a couple when your masculine and feminine side are fully lived out. So allow God to make your husband into His image instead of you attempting to make him into your image.

Be a cheerleader, not a coach.

I have really encouraged the men reading this book to take more initiative. When he does take initiative, thank him for the effort rather than critiquing him or criticizing him for the product delivered.

One time, early in our marriage, Virginia wasn't feeling well after dinner, so I suggested she go to bed and I would clean up. I did all the dishes, pulled the plug in the sink, and went to bed. The next morning I was up early, waiting for Virginia to come into the kitchen and tell me what an incredible husband I was for doing the dishes. We remember the story a bit differently, but as I remember it, she came into the kitchen and said, "Thanks so much for doing the dishes last night. Why didn't you finish the job?" I didn't hear any affirmation; all I heard was, "You did it wrong, idiot." Whenever a critique or criticism follows a compliment, the compliment is erased in our minds. She was right, I hadn't finished the job. The truth was that after I washed the last dish and put it in the drying rack, I pulled the plug and went to bed. I failed to wipe down the counter and wipe out the sink. Thus, there was dried gunk in the sink and stains on the counter.

It would have been more helpful to me for her to simply say, "Thanks so much for doing the dishes last night, I really appreciate it." *Stop.* Later in the day she could have said something like, "Thanks again for doing the dishes last night. You likely didn't even think of this, but I've found it easier if I wipe down the counter and the sink while they're still wet, rather than in the morning when everything is dry."

I truly think most wives think they are being helpful when they make suggestions. They feel they are just trying to make their husbands better. For instance, after our last child left the house, Virginia seemed to have more time to focus on my driving and took it upon herself to be "helpful."

"Do you know you are driving over the speed limit?"

"Why are you in this lane?"

"Don't you think you are a bit close to the car ahead of you?"

She was shocked when I suggested driving in separate cars to a local speaking engagement so I could be in a better frame of mind when we arrived.

To be honest, we husbands realize we often will "get it wrong." It isn't even the suggestion of how to do it differently that bothers us as much as the way the remark is made or the look that suggests we are inept or uncaring.

Sometimes, however, we don't get it as husbands. When we lived on Catalina Island, off the coast of southern California, a friend of mine planned a surprise for his wife's 40th birthday. One Friday, he picked her up from the school where she taught and whisked her to an afternoon boat headed for Long Beach.

WHENEVER A CRITIQUE OR CRITICISM FOLLOWS A COMPLIMENT, THE COMPLIMENT IS ERASED IN OUR MINDS.

As they passed their house, she asked where they were going. "*Surprise!* I'm taking you to the mainland for your 40th birthday."

"Who is watching the kids?" she asked.

"All taken care of."

"I didn't pack!"

"All taken care of: I did."

She thought, "*Great—nothing but negligees.*" They spent the weekend together at a wonderful resort and had a horrible time. All weekend she kept letting him know how much she had planned on doing over the weekend and how far behind she would be the next week.

Who was at fault for the weekend being a disaster? Certainly her husband, who after 15 years or marriage should have known she did not like surprises and was a planner to the 10th degree. But she also was at fault in not seeing or appreciating his heart that wanted to give her a wonderful, relaxing weekend.

It would have certainly been wiser for him to let her know ahead of time that in two weeks he had a weekend surprise planned and all she had to do was pack for warm weather.

We as husbands need to be more observant, and I have suggested that to the men. It would be helpful if you as wives worked at being more affirming of our efforts.

Most men live with dread of five days of the year: your anniversary, your birthday, Christmas, Valentine's Day, and if you have children, Mother's Day. We are pretty sure we will not get it right.

We can learn as husbands, but often it takes a few tries. Please encourage our efforts and any initiative we take.

> **WHEN MEN ARE TOLD THEY ARE FAILING AT WORK, THEY USUALLY WORK HARDER; WHEN THEY ARE TOLD THEY ARE FAILING AT HOME, THEY QUIT.**

He is called to lead, so let him.

After Adam and Eve sinned, God addressed Adam and said, "Because you listened to your wife . . ." This is not saying that your husband should not listen and engage with you; it means that Adam followed Eve's lead rather than listening to God and then leading Eve. And even though Adam failed at leading and protecting Eve in the Garden, God continued to call on Adam to lead. There will be times when you think you know better, and times when you do know better. But when you let your husband know in various ways that "he failed," he will likely quit leading and you will eventually resent him for it. I am not sure why this is, but when men are told they are failing at work, they usually work harder; when they are told they are failing at home, they quit. This in no way means we do not need your help. Appreciating our efforts to lead is much more helpful than pointing out our failures.

It is interesting that wives are only instructed to do two things in reference to their husbands: submit and respect. Submission has gotten a lot of bad press, but remember that you are instructed to submit "as unto the Lord." I have been pretty clear with the husbands that their authority to lead requires them always to put the interests of their wives before their own, just as Christ did for the Church. For you, I am asking you to see Jesus as your example of submission. He was not weak or a second-class citizen in any way, but He submitted to the Father: "Not my will but yours be done." I have a very strong, opinionated, talented wife. She expresses her views quite clearly—but for the most part, she allows me to lead after I have heard her input.

Often when older men are asked what makes their marriage work, they reply, "I just say 'Yes, dear.'" It may be good for a laugh, but it does not make for a good marriage. "Yes, dear" men, as they grow old, are often quiet; they follow their wife's lead; they are pleasant, but not engaging. Many times their wife drives the car, they may even walk behind her, and they let her make the decisions. It's a peaceful house—just not a vital, intimate, passionate, life-giving house. You see, he gave up living years ago.

Since husbands have been given responsibility for the home, they must also be given authority in the home. It is interesting to note that while Eve first ate the fruit in the Garden, Adam was the one held responsible for sin entering the world.

> *Therefore, just as sin came into the world through one man, and death through sin, and so death spread to all men because all sinned . . .* —Romans 5:12

Adam utterly failed in his role as leader, but God did not say, "You blew it, Adam; I am making Eve the leader." No, in essence, God said, "You blew it, Adam, but you are my man. Now get back in there and lead."

Please affirm your husband's leadership whenever you can, even when it does not seem to be the best way of doing something. Ask yourself, "Do I value being right more than strengthening my relationship with my husband?" I have found that in the atmosphere of affirmation, most men become more vulnerable and seek input from their wives.

I have asked the men to lead. I have also sought to express clearly that leadership is not dictatorship. Wise leaders seek advice from those on their team who are wiser than they. When he feels that you respect his leadership, he will be much more likely to ask for your advice.

Being respected by you is extremely important to us.

At a dinner party, I asked a group of men what they wished their wives understood about them. They almost unanimously answered, "We wish they understood that being respected by them is the

FOR MANY MEN, THE WORD THAT THEY WOULD USE TO DESCRIBE THEMSELVES WOULD BE "DISAPPOINTMENT."

greatest gift they can give us. Second, we like sex . . . That's about it!!" Most wives, if asked, would say they respect their husbands. Ask those same husbands if they feel respected by their wives, and many would say, "Not often." It often comes as a shock to wives that their behavior is read as disrespectful by their husbands. Behavior seen as disrespectful often comes in the form of questions like, "Do you know what time it is?" or "Do you know how to put the lid down?" or "Are you planning to lose weight?" or "Did you miss having your quiet time again today?"

One wife we know came home late one evening after her husband had put the children down so she could go out with the girls. She came into the house and went straight to the children's bedroom to check on them. Her first words, with an attitude, as she returned to the living room were, "I can't believe you put the summer pajamas on the kids—it's winter! What is wrong with you?" Ladies, unless you have your children sleep outdoors, it really doesn't matter what PJs they wear—your house stays 68 degrees year 'round! For heaven's sake, just thank him for watching the children!

It seems whatever we do is just not good enough. We don't do dishes right. We don't take care of ourselves as we should. We don't drive correctly.

When we asked a couple what brought them to our office for counseling, the wife blurted out, "We both work full time and he does nothing to help around the house." We expected him to be defensive or to disagree, but his response was simply, "She's right." We asked him to explain why he was not more helpful around the house. He went on to say, "When we were first married, I tried. I had dinner waiting for her when she got home from work, but she said it had too much fat in it and she would prefer cooking herself, so I let her. I offered to do the dishes, but was told I did it wrong and she would prefer doing them herself the way she wanted them done, the right way, so I let her."

He said he then offered to vacuum, thinking, "who can fail at that?" but apparently he did, and she took over the duties of vacuuming. He then foolishly tried his hand at laundry and we all know how that ended up.

"So," he repeated, "she's right, I don't do anything around the house, but not because I am not willing. It's because I am apparently just inept at everything." (Not surprisingly, this couple is now divorced.)

For many men, the word that they would use to describe themselves would be "disappointment." They feel they are a disappointment to you, they feel they often fail as a father, and they know they aren't the man of God they should be.

Your desire to help often feels like a disrespectful attempt to control.

It is significant to note that the result of sin in the Garden of Eden is that wives' desire to help will become a desire to control:

> . . . *Your desire will be for your husband . . .* —Genesis 3:16 (NIV)

The desire spoken of is not a good desire but a desire to control one's husband. Without God's intervention, women will have a tendency to undermine, overrule, and usurp the God-given leadership role of the husband. Christian author Larry Crabb puts it this way:

Submission is resisting the urge to control.
—Larry Crabb, *The Marriage Builder*, p. 119

Virginia and I were riding with some dear friends of ours when the husband pulled into a parking spot. His wife immediately said, "Why don't you park over there?" (ten spaces away), so he did.

As we walked away, he said, "If I had parked over here in the first place, she would have said, 'Why are you parking here?'" If it really is not a right or wrong, let it go.

Unfortunately, many women are clueless about this. Ask your husband to tell you each time he feels disrespected by you this week. Please don't follow his pronouncement with "That's not true!" Often what you see as "helpful hints" are seen as disrespectful statements to your husband.

When it comes to sex, we are wired differently—by God.

God made men to be visually stimulated sexually, to be aroused quickly, and to think about sex frequently. When a somewhat provocative commercial comes on TV, Virginia will say something like "Isn't that disgusting?" Honestly, that was not the first thought that came through my mind. This is not an excuse for sinful behavior by your husband, but just to alert you that his interest in sex is not inherently evil. His interest in sex does not necessarily make him a pervert, just a male!

For most men, sexual connectedness is a doorway to relationship, just as for most women relational connectedness is a doorway to physical connectedness. Here's the problem: if your husband doesn't meet your relational needs, you likely phone a girlfriend or spend time with other ladies in your small group. But your husband has only one permissible option for meeting his sexual needs and desires . . . *you!*

In the secular world, men brag about their masculinity by talking about how many women they have slept with. When a man becomes a Christian, his libido doesn't suddenly diminish. His masculinity is still somehow connected with his sexuality. For most men, sexual rejection is total rejection. When he is rejected sexually, he often thinks something must be wrong with him. For most men, pleasing their wives sexually and having their wives desire them is like the greatest thing ever.

I would encourage you to try to respond to his sexual advances, even when you are tired, have a headache, or are simply not in the mood. One woman we heard speak said the advice she was given prior to marriage was to never refuse his sexual advances, and she hadn't. Now there is a man with a smile on his face! But, *don't panic.* I have told the husbands that they are the chief servants in the bedroom as well, and they are to put your needs ahead of their own, even sexually. They are to believe that a headache is really a headache, or that you really are too tired. However, don't miss the point: if you have a headache every night for a week or more, you should see a doctor!

I would challenge you to take it to the next level by taking some initiative in the sexual area of your marriage. For the next month, initiate sex at least three times a week and see what it does for your marriage. Ask your husband to shower with you. Try being naked in bed when he crawls in. Send him a text saying you can't wait to make love with him tonight (check the addressee of the text closely before you send it). Surprise him and send the children away for the night—and then greet him in an outfit you would not wear if the children were home. Use your imagination!

Sometimes a wife feels it's her duty to show more interest in sex, so she says things like, "Do you really want me to shower with you?" or "If you need to make love tonight, I will do it—if it doesn't take too long. I'm really tired." Such statements are akin to saying to a dog, "I have this stick in my hand that I could throw. Would you really like me to throw it?" Duh! Don't make him feel like you are doing him a favor by being involved sexually. You likely wouldn't appreciate him saying "If you really need to talk, I will—if it doesn't take too long," or "Do you need me to take a walk with you? I'm working on a really important project, but if you want me to stop what I am doing I will walk with you. Just don't expect me to talk."

Be willing to have a talk with your husband about his satisfaction in this area and how the two of you could increasingly turn having sex into making love.

For us, communication tends to be functional.

Most husbands do not respond well to the 21-questions game. When I come home at night, Virginia will ask me how my day was. My answer is "Fine." That actually is a complete sentence. Virginia will then start on a litany of very annoying questions. "What do you mean, 'fine'? Who did you see? What did you do? Did you go out to lunch? Where did you go for lunch? Who did you go out with? How are they? What did you order? Who paid? You didn't have dessert, did you? . . ." I had said what I meant: the day was fine!

I have encouraged your husbands to share a bit more, but: here is the reason many men don't share. Often when they do, they get follow-up questions to every statement, or a critique on what they shared. He might say, "It was a hard day. I didn't get the raise I was expecting." Many wives would weigh in, saying something like, "Well, I hope you didn't just sit there. You did express your displeasure, didn't you, and let him know of your longstanding commitment to the company and your excellent past reviews? Did you point out that you work later than many of your fellow employees?" All he needs is, "I am so sorry. That is really unfair in my eyes, given the commitment you have made to the company. I think you're the best."

Scripture instructs us to *"encourage one another daily"* (Hebrews 3:13, NIV) and to say *"only such as is good for building up, as fits the occasion, that it may give grace to those who hear"* (Ephesians 4:29). It is easy for your communication to be discouraging, nagging, disrespectful, and not beneficial, even though you are sincerely trying to be helpful. Though we don't always show it, your affirmation and approval means the world to us.

Ask God to help you use your communication in ways that help your husband come alive.

Sometimes it seems to us husbands that children, family, friends, and activities are more important to you than we are.

Not long after we become each other's "everything," new everythings seem to creep between us. The "everythings" are often good things. It may be our jobs, our involvement in our child's classroom, our volunteering at church, clubs or small groups we are involved in—or even our children themselves.

Many a husband has felt deserted by his wife when children came along. I distinctly remember an exchange I had with a couple while emceeing a marriage conference. One of the "ice breaker" questions was "How long has it been since you have been away for a weekend together, just the two of you?" One couple said "eight years" because their daughter had said they couldn't leave her. Another couple said it had been 18 years, because they had to wait until their children were grown.

Now, I love children and think that raising them is very important, but it's not as important as keeping your marriage a priority. Scripture speaks of only one human "oneness" relationship, and it is between you and your husband. You are never called to be one with your children, your parents, your friends, or your co-workers.

Scripture is very clear that when you are married, you are to leave your mother and father and cleave to your spouse, and the two of you are to become one. Again, this does not mean that you don't care for your children or relate to your friends and parents. *But,* they are never to rank above your husband. Many men will say their wife's priorities seem to be children, parents, friends, and then husband. Make sure your vacations, holidays, and free time are not determined and defined first by doing what others wish you to do instead of what you as a couple have decided is best for you and your family.

I realize that getting away together for a weekend or even a date night can be challenging with childcare needs. I think many wives are too picky on childcare and use this as an excuse for never getting away. If the sitter doesn't harm them, leave the children with the sitter. Your children won't die if they watch TV all weekend and eat sugar snacks. Your marriage will likely die, however, if you don't take time for yourselves. Be creative and consider a short rendezvous. Go out for a quick "date lunch" or have breakfast together after dropping the kids off for school. Swap with a neighbor and have them watch your kids for an hour so your husband can come home for a bite of lunch and maybe a "quickie" if his schedule permits. (His schedule will likely permit!)

Husbands need to be affirmed in expressing their spiritual life in a way consistent with their "maleness."

We asked the couple why they were in to see us. The wife started by saying, "I am so disappointed in the spiritual depth of my husband. He only spends about 10 minutes a day in prayer and Bible reading.

If he were really serious about his walk with the Lord, he would spend at least 30 to 45 minutes with the Lord before starting his day, like I do. I mean, I have given him devotionals and everything."

IF YOU CONTINUE TO TELL YOUR HUSBAND WHAT A FAILURE HE IS SPIRITUALLY, HE WILL BECOME WHAT YOU SAY.

I finally interrupted her. "Did you say your husband spends about 10 minutes each day in personal prayer and Bible study?"

"Yes, isn't that pathetic?"

Well, I would say "remarkable." He is in the top 5% of men in our church that I know. But I will tell you, if you continue to tell your husband what a failure he is spiritually, he will become what you say.

There is no specific time, place, or pattern that scripture gives us for our personal devotional life. The goal is that we all be more conformed to the image of Christ, not that we all have the same form in our spiritual disciplines.

Again, affirming and encouraging your husband's expression of love for the Lord will reap many more rewards than you insisting that he worship like you, be in a small group like you, or read the daily reading plan you are using.

Since prayer is talking with God, don't be surprised when your husband is more "task-oriented" in his prayer life than you, the same as when he talks to everyone else. When Virginia and I pray, she starts with, "Lord, I want to thank you for the beauty of your creation we observe today. The cumulus clouds, the bright blue sky, and the roar of the ocean all remind me of your majesty . . ." It takes her 5 minutes to "get into" the prayer. I more often start with, "Lord, thanks for this day. You know the meeting I have and the game the girls have and the study Virginia is in. Please meet us all and help us to honor you." We tend to pray like we talk. God understands that. Brant Hansen, in his great book, *Blessed Are the Misfits*, points out that the prayer Jesus Himself taught us to pray takes only 25 seconds to say. Don't expect more of your husband than Jesus does.

We are wired to be the providers, so being unable to provide contributes to our sense of inadequacy.

When we were first married, I was taking home $600 per month. Our house payment was $350 a month, thus leaving us with $250 each month for everything else. It was not uncommon for us to have more month than we did money. I would come home on a Friday night and say, "Let's kick off this weekend with dinner out." Virginia would often say something like, "We don't have any money left for that." What I *heard* was, "You are such an inadequate provider, we can't even go for a stupid meal out." All she was really saying was, "We're out of money."

When a man is told or it is implied that he can't provide, it rips at his very soul. When Adam and Eve were faced with the consequences of their sin, it is interesting that Adam's consequence had to do with providing by tilling the soil. Eve's has to do with nurturing and child-birth. This is not to say that men can't be nurturing and that women can't provide, but we have seen that for most men, being removed from the provider role chafes against his design.

One other thought on this. Many wives want their husband home as if he worked at Home Depot from 9 to 5, but they want the lifestyle of an executive who works 60–80 hours a week. Talk together about finances and help each other out.

Be who you are called to be, even when he is not being who he is called to be.

A wife asked us a very sobering question recently. "Am I supposed to stay with my husband if he does not cherish me? If so, how should I respond to a man who acts as though he detests me?"

Another woman we know has a husband who suffers from a disease in such a way that he literally gets up, goes to work, comes home, and goes to bed. Should she be relegated to a life of caring for him without anything coming her way?

When we got married, most of us repeated the vows "for better, for worse, for richer, for poorer, in sickness and in health, to love and to cherish, till death do us part." Most of us only *heard* "for better . . . for richer . . . and in health."

When our expectations for marriage are not met, we have a decision to make: how are we going to live in the "new normal"? We seem to be better at doing this with our children than with our spouse. If a child has a disease or special needs that were never expected, we don't walk away. We adjust because of our love for them.

Scripture certainly gives reasons to dissolve a marriage: when repeated, unrepented infidelity occurs, when desertion of the marriage vows takes place, or when there is abuse or "hardness of heart" in such a way that it is more destructive to stay in the marriage than to leave.

The reason Jesus does not support "for any cause" raised in Matthew 19 for divorce is because our desire to avoid suffering or any unpleasantness for "any cause" could be significantly less than what God declares as reason to dissolve the covenant commitment of marriage.

So, without in any way minimizing the difficulty of situations many wives find themselves in, I would humbly suggest these actions.

- Ask God to be to you what your husband has failed to be or is incapable of being.
- Align yourself with a healthy Christian fellowship and allow women there to come alongside you.
- Ask God to help you be all you should be to your husband in the situation you find yourself in.
- Live with him as though he is incapable of change.
- Love him as though he has completely changed.
- Pray for God to strengthen your heart and, where possible, to change his heart.

A friend of ours lived faithfully with and cared well for his wife who was severely depressed (and in and out of mental institutions) for most of their marriage. Once, as the two of them were talking together, the wife told her husband, "I don't think I would still be alive if it weren't for your love." The husband immediately responded, "And I wouldn't be the man I am today if it weren't for you."

This friend wrote us an email describing his marriage, and ended with the following story and a comment. I share it with you as well:

> There is an old story of an older missionary couple that came back to the States on a steamship, after a long and faithful career of serving God invisibly and without much reward overseas. They were at the rail of the ship as it came to its berth, and there was much fanfare and commotion there on the dock to greet a famous dignitary who was coming home. The man mumbled something to his wife about how they weren't getting any kind of a welcoming or recognition. His wife paused a moment and then said, "But honey, we're not home yet."
>
> This world is not all there is. This world is upside down. But, one day, your wife will be fully alive, and so will you. One day. So keep hoping. As you live in the messiness of the present, keep hoping for the wonder of the future. It is beyond what you can imagine. So keep hoping.

Some of you are living in the "messiness of the present." Keep being faithful and keep hoping. God can use you in your husband's life in miraculous ways and use your life as an example to the many who are watching you, wondering if the Gospel really works. May God give you strength and joy in the journey.

So, Ladies

As we stated at the beginning of this chapter, some of you have gotten this book in hopes of fixing your husband—and you may be tempted to tell him he needs to read it or to tell him what he should do. I would suggest that if any of what has been shared in this chapter rings true in your own life, please simply live it out in the hope he will ask you, "What has happened to you?" Or, you might say to him, if true, "I purchased a book in hopes that you would read it and it would help you—and what I found is that it has helped me! So I want to apologize for the ways I have not been the wife God has called me to be in our marriage."

We had just finished a marriage seminar in Tehachapi, California, and I met a couple in the lobby that had been serving refreshments for the seminar. When I thanked them for their service, the wife said, "No, the thanks is ours. I made my husband come this weekend against his will. I thought he really needed to hear how he was failing as a husband. Well, the tables got turned. I realized I have failed as a wife in almost all the areas you addressed this weekend. He is always inviting me to go away for the weekend to fish with him and I have never gone, saying 'I just don't like it. I would rather stay home by myself than be fishing with you.' Well, we are going on a fishing trip next week."

I don't know what your husband's "fishing trip" is, but I can assure you that if you start responding more to his desires, I think you will find you will have a husband more like the one you have longed for.

(It has now been just over a year since the conference in Tehachapi. Virginia and I just returned from speaking there again. As we were talking to the pastor and his wife, I asked how the "fishing couple" was doing. There was a brief hesitation, and then we were told the wife had passed away recently from an aggressive form of cancer. We never know when will be the last opportunity to "go fishing" with our spouse.)

It is interesting that the apostle Peter, talking about how to win unbelieving husbands, tells wives to win them "without a word."

Likewise, wives, be subject to your own husbands, so that even if some do not obey the word, they may be won without a word by the conduct of their wives, when they see your respectful and pure conduct. —1 Peter 3:1–2

Some husbands say that when their wife "got religious," their marriage suffered. Knowing Christ should certainly change your marriage, but for the better. You are now a "new creation." You should be more enjoyable to be around, more encouraging, less nagging, more respectful, a better lover.

On a recent trip to Uganda where we gave a marriage conference, our "driver" attended the conference with his wife. After the conference he asked his wife what she had learned. She replied, "I am not going to tell you, I am going to show you." A week later we asked our driver how it was going for him since the conference. With a huge grin on his face he shared that his wife was showing him what she learned. Win them without a word.

ONE LAST STORY

Our daughter Julie and her husband, Derek, lived in Mbale, Uganda, for the first four years of their marriage, where Derek was the Executive Director of the CURE Children's Hospital. The hospital treats children with hydrocephalus and spina bifida. The hospital not only serves the children, but also cares for the mamas while the children are at the hospital. The spiritual directors at the hospital teach crafts to the mamas and spend time praying with them and sharing the Gospel with them. The hospital has an incredible record of saving children's lives, but occasionally a child's sickness will be so advanced when they arrive at the hospital that it is not possible to save the child's life.

This was the case for one young boy who died in surgery. During the stay, his mama had become a believer, but she went back to her tribe grieving the loss of her son. Two weeks later, there was a man banging on the hospital compound gate. The guards were fearful when they discovered the man was the father of the young boy who had passed. They knew the tribe had an eye-for-an-eye mentality and were fearful he was coming to get revenge for the death of his son. Finally the man yelled to the guards, "My wife was here with my son two weeks ago, and whatever you did to my wife, I want you to do it for me."

Ladies, that is my greatest prayer for you, to live in such a way with your husband that he will say, "Whatever happened to you is what I want to happen to me. I really do want to learn to love you like Christ, even if I ain't no Jesus."

About the Author

Dr. Paul Friesen has been married for 42 years to his wife, Virginia, and they are the parents of three young adult girls, two of whom are now married to wonderful, Godly men. Their middle daughter is living fully for Christ as a single woman and trusting God for His best.

Paul has been involved in Family Ministries for over 45 years through family camps, church staff positions, speaking, consulting, and writing.

Paul and Virginia are the founders of Home Improvement Ministries (www.HIMweb.org), a non-profit organization dedicated to equipping individuals and churches to better encourage marriages and families in living out God's design for healthy relationships. As the lead resource couple at Home Improvement Ministries, Paul and Virginia regularly speak at marriage, men's, and women's conferences in the US and internationally, as well as local family and parenting seminars, and have an ongoing ministry with professional athletes.

Paul has authored over fifteen books and curriculums on parenting and marriage, including *Letters to My Daughters, In Our Image, Before You Save the Date*, and along with Virginia, *The Marriage App*. He has a doctorate in Marriage and Family Therapy and a master's degree in Family Ministry, both from Gordon-Conwell Theological Seminary.

Paul and Virginia's greatest joy in life is knowing that their children are "walking in the truth."

Other resources available from Home Improvement Ministries:

Parenting
Raising a Trailblazer, Virginia Friesen. (book)
Parenting by Design, Paul and Virginia Friesen. (DVD series, with study guide)
The Father's Heart, Paul and Virginia Friesen. (DVD series, with study guide)

Dating and Engagement
Letters to My Daughters, Paul Friesen. (book)
Letters to My Daughters Discussion Guide, Paul Friesen. (study guide)
Before You Save the Date, Paul Friesen. (book)
So You Want to Marry My Daughter?, Paul Friesen. (book)
Engagement Matters, Paul and Virginia Friesen. (study guide)

Marriage
The Marriage App, Paul and Virginia Friesen. (book)
The Marriage App, Paul and Virginia Friesen. (software)
Restoring the Fallen, Earl and Sandy Wilson, Paul and Virginia Friesen, Larry and Nancy Paulson. (book)
Marriage, Culture, and Scripture, Paul and Virginia Friesen. (book)
In Our Image, Paul and Virginia Friesen. (study guide)
Jesus on Marriage, Paul and Virginia Friesen. (study guide)
Recapturing Eden, Paul and Virginia Friesen. (DVD series, with study guide)
Created in God's Image, Paul and Virginia Friesen. (DVD series, with study guide)
The Delight of Sacrificial Love in Marriage, Paul and Virginia Friesen. (CD; recorded talk with PDF outline)
The Delight of Experiencing Love and Respect in Marriage, Paul and Virginia Friesen. (CD; recorded talk with PDF outline)
The Delight of Uniqueness in Marriage, Paul and Virginia Friesen. (CD; recorded talk with PDF outline)
The Delight of Sexual Intimacy in Marriage, Paul and Virginia Friesen. (CD; recorded talk with PDF outline)

Discipleship
Gospel Revolution, Gabriel Garcia. (book)

For more information about Home Improvement Ministries or to order any of our products, please contact us:

Call: 781-275-6473
Email: info@himweb.org
Write: Home Improvement Ministries
         213 Burlington Road, Suite 101-B
         Bedford, MA 01730 USA
Online: www.HIMweb.org/books (for the online bookstore)
         www.HIMweb.org/speak (to book speakers)
         www.HIMweb.org/fb   (to reach us on Facebook)